AN INDIAN AMONG LOS INDÍGENAS

AN INDIAN AMONG LOS INDÍGENAS

A NATIVE TRAVEL MEMOIR

Ursula Pike

HEYDAY, BERKELEY, CALIFORNIA

Library of Congress Cataloging-in-Publication Data

Names: Pike, Ursula, 1968- author.
Title: An Indian among los Indígenas / Ursula Pike.
Description: Berkeley, California : Heyday, [2021]
Identifiers: LCCN 2020030725 (print) | LCCN 2020030726 (ebook) | ISBN 9781597145275 (hardcover) | ISBN 9781597145282 (ebook)
Subjects: LCSH: Pike, Ursula, 1968---Travel--Bolivia. | Peace Corps (U.S.)--Biography. | Peace Corps (U.S.)--Bolivia--History--20th century. | Karok women--Biography. | Indians of South America--Bolivia--Social conditions. | Indians of North America--California--Social conditions. | Bolivia--Colonization.
Classification: LCC HC60.5 .P53 2021 (print) | LCC HC60.5 (ebook) | DDC 362.6283/9998084 [B]--dc23
LC record available at https://lccn.loc.gov/2020030725
LC ebook record available at https://lccn.loc.gov/2020030726

Cover Photo: Raúl Barrios
Endsheet Photo: Valentina Alvarez
Cover Design: Ashley Ingram
Interior Design/Typesetting: Ashley Ingram

Published by Heyday
P.O. Box 9145, Berkeley, California 94709
(510) 549-3564
heydaybooks.com

Printed in East Peoria, Illinois, by Versa Press, Inc.

10 9 8 7 6 5 4 3 2 1

FSC
www.fsc.org
MIX
Paper from responsible sources
FSC® C005010

Contents

Preface

Brooklyn Elementary School in southeast Portland, Oregon, had a special Thanksgiving celebration the year I was in third grade. Earlier that week, a man came to the school to teach us about the potlatch tradition of the Pacific Northwest Indians. This middle-aged white man overenunciated in the way adults do when they are explaining very important things to children. *Potlatch* came from a Chinook word meaning "to give," and although it sounded like "potluck," it was different. A traditional potlatch ceremony included feasting and gift giving. The more a family or a chief could share at the potlatch, the more important they were. The giving was the important part. Sharing their wealth also cemented important connections between families.

I had never heard of a potlatch. I am a member of the Karuk Tribe, from the steep mountains near the California-Oregon border, but I had also never ridden a horse, shot an arrow, or slept in a teepee—things I thought all Indians were supposed to have done.★

★ I use the following terms interchangeably for the Indigenous people of North and South America: Native, Native American, Indian, American Indian, and Indigenous people. Whenever possible, I will use specific tribal names such as Karuk, Cherokee, Quechua, and so on.

Our teachers decided that each class would have our own pot-latch before going on break, so we made headbands and attached construction-paper feathers. Some of the girls braided each other's hair. My mother almost never braided my hair even though it was long and straight, because of enormous tangles I never let her brush out. All the students and the teachers sat on the gym's wood floor in a big circle. The man played a hand drum slowly and told a story. I sat on the hard floor, thinking of what I could give as part of the potlatch. I was looking forward to the Thanksgiving break because my mom, my sister, and I were driving to my grandparents' house in Daly City, California. We often stopped in Yreka, the half-way point of the eight-hour drive, where my auntie Mary always greeted us warmly at the door no matter what time we knocked.

"Does anyone have any gifts they would like to give?" the man asked the circle. I nearly dislocated my shoulder in an attempt to be the first one to raise my hand. I was eager to show that I had absorbed the lesson of the potlatch and could perform the version of nativeness he had presented to us.

He gave me the nod and I stood up. Making elaborate hand gestures in hopes that they added to the realness of my performance, I offered an imaginary chicken to my friend across the circle. I watched the man the whole time I was talking, wanting him to affirm that I was doing it correctly. My friend on the other side of the room looked at me with confusion in her eyes.

"Say thank you," the man told her. She mumbled her gratitude for the nonexistent chicken. Standing in front of the class was embarrassing, but I was also uncomfortable because I knew I was performing an identity that looked nothing like my actual life. There was no confusion in my mind about being Karuk, but up there in front of my classmates, I thought I had to act the way he told me Indians acted. I understood that there was the real life I lived and then there was the version of American Indian everyone expected. When the exchange was over, I sat down with relief. Other children stood up and offered imaginary gifts to each other as the man coached them through the exchange. When the potlatch finally ended, I left the gym quickly, happy to be released into my real life.

My family repeated stories of Spanish, Irish, and even Cherokee ancestors, but the language my grandmother spoke to her mother was Karuk, and the culture I was taught to claim was Karuk. Unlike my grandmother, I didn't grow up near the confluence of the Klamath and Salmon Rivers. My playgrounds were in the cities of Oregon and Washington State, and I learned to ride my bike in the parking lot of a Laundromat in Portland. I know the sometimes-bitter flavor of *xuun*—a traditional acorn porridge—but I don't know how to gather acorns.

Half of what I know about my tribe comes from the stories my grandmother told me and the songs that were sung around a campfire on the river. The other half comes from books written by anthropologists. However, all of my knowledge about being an urban Indian growing up in a city comes from my lived experience. It comes from attending Portland's Delta Park powwow on the flat space off Interstate 5, where I played tag with other kids until it was too dark to see. It comes from hearing my mother's stories about working for the Bureau of Indian Affairs on reservations throughout the Pacific Northwest. I knew Native construction workers, tribal council members, fry cooks, and botanists. My understanding of what it meant to be Native also came from sitting in a student meeting during college where American Indians from different tribes, all with their own traditions, planned a powwow. My experiences and these people were never represented in the books I read or movies I saw, but they were whom I thought of when I heard the word *Indian*.

American Indian was the box I checked when I applied to college and on my Peace Corps application. When I went to Bolivia as a twenty-five-year-old Peace Corps volunteer, I knew it was a country full of Indigenous people. I wanted to help Indians. But I didn't realize that helping people is difficult. The understanding that the giver is better off than the receiver in some absolute sense hangs in the air above the transaction. And to be certain, it is a transaction. As in the exchange of those potlatch gifts, the giver expects something in return for her gift even if it is only a mumbled thank you. Trying to help people in another culture adds a level of complexity to the exchange because not every culture values the same things. I didn't understand how the "help" offered by colonizers, missionaries, and nations that preceded me cast a long shadow over all attempts at assistance.

I went to Bolivia assuming I would have connections with Indigenous Bolivians because of our shared identity as Indigenous people. All those powwow planning meetings in college with my Paiute and Yakima classmates included disagreements over everything from who should carry the flags for grand entry to the type of frybread we would serve, but we accepted that we shared a connection. In Bolivia, I learned about the similarities in the history and experiences of Indigenous people in North and South America. In South America, the Spanish launched a brutal campaign to subjugate and eradicate the Indigenous people in what would become Bolivia. On the West Coast of North America, the Spanish established a mission system with the intention of subjugating and eradicating the Indigenous people in what would become California.

El oro y la plata, gold and silver, were the reason fortune seekers from Europe came to California and South America. The Quechua and Aymara, the two largest Indigenous groups in Bolivia, had not been allowed to speak their own languages in school in exactly the same way that my grandmother and her siblings were required to speak English instead of Karuk.

When I finished training and moved out into the countryside, I was uncertain about my ability to do something meaningful. Most volunteers struggled to figure out what to do, but part of my struggle was knowing I followed in the footsteps of Western colonizers and missionaries who had also claimed they were there to help. The two years turned out nothing like what I had expected. When I boarded my return flight to the US, I didn't feel the deep sense of satisfaction about what I had done as I had believed I would.

Upon returning to the United States, I looked for stories that would help make sense of what I had experienced. There were no books by Native Americans who served in one of the predominantly Indigenous countries like Guatemala, Peru, and Ecuador. There were few books by African Americans who had served in Africa or Asian Americans who had served in Asian countries. Occasionally I would stumble on evidence that people of color had been volunteering with the Peace Corps since the agency started in 1961, but it felt like a secret.

When I sat down to turn the eight journals I filled during my time in Bolivia into this book, I thought of my favorite travel books, such as Robin Davidson's *Tracks* chronicling her camel trek across the Australian Outback and Moritz Thomsen's *Living Poor* recounting a farmer's move to Ecuador. These are my most dog-eared, repeatedly read books. In high school, I devoured P. J. O'Rourke's travel stories in *Rolling Stone* with his now cringe-worthy descriptions of Central American women with breasts that looked like the melons they carried on their heads. An economic development professor assigned Robert Klitgaard's *Tropical Gangsters: One Man's Experience with Development and Decadence in Deepest Africa*. His story of travel, exotic cultures, and ineffectual development projects read like an economic *Heart of Darkness*, and I loved it.

Yet, as much as I loved these books, I never saw myself in them. I couldn't identify with the author because it was always a white person with enough privilege and resources to leave the world of work and travel for months at a time in another country. As much as my teenage self hoped for breasts like melons, I didn't identify with the people in the countries these writers were visiting because their accounts were comically one-dimensional. The travel magazines I read would often have glossy pictures of Indigenous women sitting next to bright fruits and vegetables as if they were simply another colorful part of the landscape.

A 1921 essay by Yankton Sioux writer Zitkála-Šá titled "An Indian Teacher among Indians" exploring her time as a teacher at the Carlisle Indian School gave me an example to follow. Zitkála-Šá attended an Indian school as a child, and despite mixed emotions about her own experience, she returned to teach, hoping her work would help "the Indian race." The US government established Indian residential schools like Carlisle to "Americanize" Native Americans. Eventually, Zitkála-Šá resigned when it became impossible to ignore that the school's real purpose was to make white settlers feel superior for bestowing charity on "the children of savage warriors" instead of actually helping the children. My experience in Bolivia was different from Zitkála-Šá's, but the conflict of being both connected to and distanced from the objects of the charity work was familiar to me in a way I had never seen. The idea that the real beneficiaries of service work were the service workers themselves was a radical thought I had never dared to consider.

Every person who writes about real life in the genre called nonfiction must confront her commitment to the truth and be transparent about what was changed. To write this book, I used research, photographs and videos from 1994 through 1996, and conversations with Bolivians and former volunteers I knew during these years. I used the eight journals that I filled with my observations while I was there. I reconstructed my experience as completely and honestly as I could. Part of that reconstruction involved condensing timelines and re-creating conversations. My process was similar to what museums do when they construct a T-Rex fossil display. They don't have every part of the dinosaur's body and have to mold bones and vertebra from plaster. Adding the re-created parts gives a more complete picture of the creature. I did the same thing, but with words.

Writing about my experience in the Peace Corps still feels a little disrespectful twenty years later. Who am I to tell a story that does not look like the accepted narrative about service and charity? I feel like my nine-year-old self, standing up on a fall afternoon at Brooklyn Elementary, speaking my truth about what giving meant to me rather than saying what I thought I was supposed to say. Although I see more African American and Hispanic faces in the Peace Corps marketing and recruitment materials since my time in Bolivia, and the demographics of volunteers is a bit more diverse, books about the experience by people of color who were volunteers are still hard to find. And, at least when I began writing this story, I still hadn't seen any books or essays examining the experiences of a Native volunteer serving in an Indigenous country. Bolivia is also still relatively unknown despite recent news coverage, and few North Americans could find it on a map of South America. I wrote this book because the story of an American Indian Peace Corps volunteer who struggled while serving in an Indigenous country—my story—was missing from the library.

1

A la Llegada — Upon Arrival

I arrived in La Paz as four rum and Cokes joined forces with an altitude-induced headache. The other volunteers in the group had accepted the airline's complimentary drinks, and I assumed this was what people did on international flights. Now I stood in the tiny airport that teetered on the rim of the bowl-shaped valley of the city, feeling exhausted and unprepared. Wood-paneled walls didn't keep out the chilly air blowing across the high plateau. The T-shirt I had put on the night before in Miami provided no warmth. I forced myself to stand up straight despite wanting to lie down under something soft and warm. It was 7 a.m., and I was thirteen thousand feet above sea level.

I stepped into a quickly forming line leading to a Bolivian immigration official. His pale pockmarked face and broad unsmiling cheeks made me wonder whether he was part Indian. Native. Indigenous. Bolivia had four million Indigenous people. That was almost twice as many Natives as in the United States. In Bolivia,

Indians were the majority. I bit my lip to keep from grinning.

The Bolivian official scanned passports without a greeting or a smile, quickly looking at each person's face, then back at the passport. I stepped in front of the table where he sat and pulled my stiff passport out of the fanny pack my mother had given me before I left Oregon. Behind him was a shawl-sized painting of the red, yellow, and green Bolivian flag.

The other volunteers shuffled toward the immigration official. I had met them only forty-eight hours earlier, but I already knew exactly how many brown people were in the group. It was a tally I always made. A cute Latina from Texas, a midcareer Mexicano, a bleary-eyed Puerto Rican man, an athletic Filipina from California, and a broad-shouldered Filipino who was quiet except for the occasional self-deprecating joke. I didn't like the term *minority*, but in this case we were. The remaining twenty volunteers looked like those combinations of Western and Eastern European identities that qualify as white in the United States. Did anyone wonder what I was? My dark brown hair and olive skin gave me a vaguely ethnic look. Teachers and curious grocery clerks usually guessed Hispanic or maybe Greek. My identity was a tailless donkey they had to pin the right kind of brown to.

The immigration official looked up at my face and then down at my passport. I was excited to be standing in front of a Bolivian for the first time, but the formality of the moment made me nervous. His thick eyebrows moved up and down as he scrutinized me. Then he stamped it, handed it back to me, and reached for the next one. That wasn't what I had expected.

"Thank you for coming to my country. I can tell you are more serious than any of these gringos," said No One. I looked around at the other officials. Didn't my sincerity show through my olive skin?

Maybe it was too early in the morning. Maybe they were rushed. I waited an extra moment to give him a chance for a second look or a nod of his head. Certainly, the Bolivians would eventually recognize that I was different from the others arriving from the United States that day. They would see that because I was an American Indian, we shared a connection. Coming to a country like Bolivia, a country full of Native people, had been the secret wish held in my heart as I filled in the spaces on the Peace Corps application. Couldn't the Bolivians see that we shared a connection? Couldn't they see that my commitment was more meaningful because I was Native? The person behind me sighed, and I reluctantly moved forward.

The training group's luggage sat in a heap on the floor. My backpack, which had seemed so big in the REI outlet store back in Portland, now looked ridiculously small. The tiny straps and water-resistant pockets held two years' worth of tightly packed clothes and supplies. As the other volunteers pulled their luggage from the pile, I tried to recall who everyone was. Even after ice-breakers and introductions, I could not remember anyone's name.

Bursting leather suitcase—the athletic girl from California.

Floral-print handbag—Latina chick from Texas.

Worn North Face backpack—blond guy from Minnesota who had been smiling nonstop for two days.

The woman from Texas pulled another suitcase and more floral-print bags from the pile. Her name was Laura. The impracticality of her luggage choice made me love her. I had found my first friend. I hadn't known what to bring, but had assumed everyone else had it all figured out. Laura must have brought everything she owned in case she needed it. She was an interior designer from El Paso, which sounded exotic to me, but she assured me it wasn't. With a

Marilyn Monroe figure and the longest eyelashes I had ever seen, she was glamorous and the opposite of what I expected a Peace Corps volunteer to look like.

"Don't tell anyone, but I'm not fluent in Spanish," she confessed over beers in Miami. Her mother taught her to speak English without an accent. We'd both been raised by mothers who taught their children to be proud of their heritage without appearing too "ethnic."

"I won't, if you don't tell them I'm too fat," I said. She laughed long enough to erase the embarrassment attached to the invitation letter informing me that I was three pounds above the acceptable weight for my height. For months, I worried there would be a scale at the airport with a trap door underneath ready to whoosh me back home if the wrong number appeared.

We followed the blond volunteer with the smooth southern drawl who was leading the way into the main part of the terminal. Round faces and short women wearing bulky skirts were everywhere. Long, dark braids hung down from black bowler hats that sat askew on their heads. They were Aymara women, Indigenous celebrities. Like the immigration official, none of them gave me a second look. I hoped that once I was apart from this gaggle of North Americans, I would be noticed.

In the parking lot on the high plateau where the airport stood, the sun felt a few miles away. I shaded my eyes with my hand and squinted to see a rumbling school bus waiting to take us to the Peace Corps offices. That's when I saw Mt. Illimani. The mountain's triple peaks loomed over the valley beneath us. It peeped over the rim of La Paz like the Abominable Snowmonster in the *Rudolph the Red-Nosed Reindeer* Christmas special. The wind pushed into the side of my face, whipping my hair from the barrette holding it down. Between the sunshine and the frozen wind, I was now fully awake. My heart beat faster from a combination of altitude and excitement. I was finally standing in Bolivia.

Seven months earlier, I called the recruiter in Seattle during my coffee break. The college degree I worked so hard for hadn't led to any jobs beyond temporary positions in offices that were as depressing and bleakly corporate as this one. The file clerks on the seventeenth floor shared one hideous black phone, and although I wasn't supposed to use it for personal calls, I couldn't wait any longer. I had to know whether the Peace Corps wanted me. After eighteen months of filling out forms, begging forgotten professors to write reference letters, and doctor's exams, I was almost ready to give up. Almost. Outside the windows, a line of gray clouds made it impossible to see Mt. Hood, the lopsided beauty I had been look-ing at for most of my twenty-five years.

The phone rang, and I finally had the recruiter on the line. We had never met in person. I didn't want to sound desperate, but I really needed her to tell me something positive. When my boss told me there might be a future for me at the insurance agency, I knew it was time for me to move on. I didn't want a secure position moving pieces of paper around the seventeenth floor. The Peace Corps had been the next step I had counted on since high school. Adventure, travel, and service in one government-funded package seemed too good to be true. Why didn't everyone join? But with an economics degree from a low-ranked state school and experience wiping noses at the college day-care center, I was not at the top of the Peace Corps' recruitment list. My boyfriend submitted his application the same week I did. His physics degree from a private college gained him acceptance with such speed that he barely had time to pack his Moosewood cookbooks into his VW van before departing for Africa. I wasn't sure what was more heartbreaking: that he had no qualms about leaving me or that the Peace Corps welcomed him into its ranks with such haste.

"Do you have any news for me, maybe?" I asked the recruiter. I had no time for small talk. There had been so many rejections from other volunteer positions in Africa and Asia. Each time, I was told I was not qualified. I had the wrong degree, the wrong experience, and the wrong life to pursue this dream.

"Why yes I do, and I think you're going to like it." I could tell she was smiling. I was too nervous to smile. "You're going to Bolivia." I almost dropped the phone on the desk when she said this. I couldn't believe it was finally happening.

"What was different this time?" I asked her. Was it the two years of Spanish I took in college? Or maybe all the hours I spent in the library studying to bring my GPA up?

"To be honest, it was…" She hesitated. "It's because you're an American Indian," she said in a rush of words. It wasn't the answer I had expected. Gratitude and resentment mixed in my throat. I swallowed.

"Peace Corps needs more minorities." Her voice was cheerful but forced. If I had known that was the key to an invitation, I would have tied a burning bundle of sage to my application or sent it wrapped in a Pendleton blanket months ago. I glanced at the clock on the wall. Break time was ending—this life-changing moment needed to end in less than five minutes.

"I remember when I first went to El Salvador," she said. Then she began telling me a story about plantains, or it might have been children. Honestly, I wasn't listening. I had the information I wanted; I was ready to get off the phone. And I couldn't forget what she had said. *Peace Corps needs more minorities.* I could have told them that. In eighteen months of attending recruiting events, every returned volunteer I met was white. Most of the potential volunteers getting recruited at these events were white. They needed me as much as I needed them. But, of course, I couldn't say that. Any reaction other than impossible-to-mistake gratitude would be seen as bad form. I thanked her and told her how excited I was.

"I'll be honest—this is probably the only invitation I'll be able to get for you," the recruiter said. Her voice was flat and breathy; maybe she was trying to keep people on the other end from hearing what she said. Bolivia was my one chance. By the time I hung up, my hand was wet with sweat. I slumped onto the table with relief.

The simple story I told my friends and family that night did not include everything the recruiter had said. I wasn't quite sure how to tell the complicated truth. But the overnight flight to La Paz wouldn't leave for another six months. In that time, I would still have to pay for rent, food, college loans, and a $400 credit card bill. Six more months of retrieving files and pushing carts full of paperwork between office cubicles awaited me. I wasn't sure what Bolivia would be like, but I couldn't wait to begin the adventure.

2

Cochabamba

Bolivia was isolated—isolated by mountains and expanses of sparsely populated, rugged terrain. It was a landlocked country that lost access to the Pacific Ocean in 1904 after a war with Chile. In Bolivia, the Andes Mountains broke into two separate ranges and continued bumping along South America into Chile and Argentina. There were vistas of snow-capped mountains with tranquil llamas silently chewing in the foreground. But Bolivia also had mountains of jagged orange and slate jutting toward the sky. Centuries of wind and rain erosion had revealed layers of red and gray minerals. Roads were built around the treeless, steep mountains because there was no going over them. In Potosi, the high-altitude, bone-chilling city whose silver deposits inspired the hot greed of Spaniards, the hard brown shape of Cerro Rico (literally, Rich Mountain) could be seen from every narrow street and open plaza.

Bolivia was also home to the world's largest salt flat, Salar De Uyuni, an expanse of horizon-skimming whiteness that stretched for mile after barren mile. An Aymara Indian story explained that the mountains surrounding the salt flat were once giants. One of the giants deserted his wife for another woman while his wife was breastfeeding their child. She cried and cried. The tears mixed with the milk and ran down her chest in white streams, covering the vast area between them. When it was dry, the sun reflected off the salty whiteness. Light-skinned tourists were burned to a shade of pink not unlike the flamingos that flocked there to mate every November. During the rainy season, a thin layer of water accumulated on the surface and turned the salt flat into a giant mirror that reflected the sky and erased the horizon.

Tourists were drawn to the remoteness, to the myth of Bolivia's savage purity. It let them prove they were travelers and not tourists. Tourists ordered frozen blue drinks from the hotel bar. Travelers, by contrast, rode buses without shocks for fifty cents while suppressing their explosive diarrhea, proving their heartiness. What about the grandmother seated next to the traveler? She had been riding the same bus for twenty years. The bus was luxurious compared to the back of the truck she had ridden the previous twenty years. Would she see a difference between a traveler and a tourist? Or would she simply see a gringo riding through her country as though it were a roller coaster?

The eastern border of Bolivia pressed up against the backside of Brazil. The rivers from that region flowed into the Amazon basin, and the jungles were full of the world's largest rodents, thick vegetation, and piranha. By the 1990s when I was there, the Eastern Lowlands were one of the poorest regions of Bolivia. Giant cattle ranches with few cattle remained. Many hid processing operations that turned the coca leaves grown nearby into cocaine for North American snorting. We were told it was a dangerous, messy part of the country, thick with yellow-fever-infected mosquitoes and no volunteers. But the tribes in these lowlands had built causeways that stretched for miles, controlling the water and enabling large communities to exist well before the Spanish showed up.

The mountains, the Salar, and the thick jungles all made Bolivia a difficult place to explore. The isolation and remoteness helped the Quechua, Aymara, Guarani, and other tribes maintain their culture and language for centuries. Some of the tribes managed to stay hidden until the twentieth century. But the riches in the ground itself worked against their efforts. Gold, tin, rubber, mahogany, cocaine, lithium, and even the water drew Westerners who did what they do: explore, infect, desiccate. But those Natives were still there, speaking their languages, dancing, and feeding themselves and their children.

On the fifth day, we flew to Cochabamba, a city in central Bolivia, and another snowy peak on the horizon reminded me that we were still in the Andes. Cochabamba reclined across a broad valley, dipping her toes in Lake Alalay on the southern edge of the city. An enormous white statue of Jesus stood firmly on a low hill, reaching out to the city with his arms open and eyes staring forward. It was still winter in the Southern Hemisphere, but the valley was warm enough that I could relax my shoulders instead of hunching up against the cold. For the first time since arriving, my breathing was full and deep.

I was eager to get out, ask people for directions in Spanish, and crinkle a Bolivian dollar between my fingers, but was led onto a bus heading to the training center. Out the window, I saw women walking down the street in flouncy *pollera* skirts that shifted with each step, and the chubby babies they carried in bright fabric tied around their shoulders. I learned that these were *cholitas*, women who wore traditional clothing such as the ruffled skirts, hats, and shawls. They were Indigenous or, like many Natives in the US, had mixed Indigenous and European background. In La Paz, cholitas wore the tiny black bowlers; but in Cochabamba, their hats were white with wide brims. The way these women took things brought by colonialists and made them their own reminded me of the tobacco lids that North American Natives used to make jingle dresses.

Quechuas were the largest Indigenous group in Bolivia, and this valley was their home. "Only a small percentage of *Cochabambinos* are of pure Indian extraction," my guidebook told me. International travelers preferred the familiar version of Indian—brown faces framed with long, dark braids—because it matched their ideas of how Indigenous Bolivians were supposed to look. The same thing happened in the US, where curious people asked me, "How Indian are you?" as though I were a breed of dog they were considering buying if my lineage was pure. Native people in Bolivia had skin tones from deep brown to pale and wore both traditional clothes and whatever their mother bought them last Christmas. In Bolivia, almost everyone had some Indigenous blood.

The bus turned into a wide road with more cars. We passed rows of low brick houses topped with corrugated tin roofs, lining unpaved roads leading up into the mountains on the edge of the city. Dust and pollution floated above the city in a thin brown cloud. Every other vehicle was a minivan packed with people who bounced when the tires hit a pothole. The bus stopped, and a willowy man waved his hand above his head, then pulled the tall metal gate open onto a small, treeless courtyard, where we were greeted with handshakes and hugs by the staff. On the other side of the sunbaked courtyard was a large, bright room with a row of windows revealing a small garden, trees, and a volleyball net. I wanted to learn everything, to speak the language, to understand the culture. Most of all, I wanted the Bolivians in this room, the instructors and the staff, to see me as someone who was like them. I didn't want to look like a grinning fool, but it was too late, and I smiled so wide my cheeks bumped into my eye sockets.

The Bolivian family who would host me for the next three months came forward. "Mucho gusto conocerte" (Nice to meet you), said Bonnie, the mother. As she stepped in close to kiss my cheek, I smelled wood smoke and soap. My first attempt at the traditional Bolivian greeting—shaking hands, then air-kissing each cheek, followed by immediately patting the outside of the person's shoulder—was imperfect, and I might have shaken her hand too vigorously. Bonnie's nine-year-old daughter, Rosa, and her teenage daughter, Morelia, looked at the ground or around the room as they shook my hand.

"Listo para salir?" (Ready to go?), Bonnie asked. I wished I knew how to say "After you" in Spanish, but I didn't, so I simply said yes and followed them out the door. As we walked on the narrow dirt path between two empty fields, I tried to memorize every rock and dog turd because I had to find my way back there the next day. The powdery dust on the path turned my boots the same color as the earth. Morelia pointed out roads that led to a nearby restaurant, but I struggled to carry on a conversation.

How different this was from being in a classroom and repeating dialogue from a book. In college, I learned Spanish during the day from glitchy videos, while in the evening I attended student-organized meetings where stories of massacres and revolutions happening in real time in Central America were translated in front of me from Spanish to English. The speakers were often Indigenous women imploring us to get the US government out of their country, to explain that millions of our tax dollars were being spent to keep dictators in power. During these presentations, I was usually silent, but wondered whether there was a way for me to help communities like theirs, to show them there were people from the United States who respected their humanity.

Bonnie and the girls led me across a wide two-lane road where minivans with barely functioning mufflers sped by, and suddenly we stood in front of an unimpressive adobe building.

"Bienvenido." Ernesto welcomed us into the front room of the house. His smile was reserved, a reflection of the smile on the face of his older daughter. He rested his hand on the fleshy shoulder of their son, an almost teenage boy standing in front of him. Inside the house was a one-room store where pocketbook-sized bags of detergent, individual rolls of purple toilet paper, coils of pasta, and stacks of red sardine cans lined the walls. We passed into a dimly lit room, and my eyes took a moment to adjust. Rooms surrounded the courtyard at the center of the house in a style I had seen in Mexico. I loved the interior courtyards of these homes because, like any good introvert, I preferred to be somewhere hidden.

"El baño…," the father said as he motioned toward a door on the far wall. Outside, I saw a small outhouse, just big enough for a toilet and a roll of paper. It was new and had smooth cement walls. The smile on Ernesto's face widened, and I knew I was supposed to be impressed. I had been in enough outhouses to know this was a good one. The seat was still white, and the smell was hardly noticeable.

"Qué bueno," I said, looking the structure up and down. The family had built the latrine specifically to be able to host volunteers like me. We volunteers required special places to shit. Each host family had to agree to a minimum of accommodations, but a sit-down latrine like this was more than the bare minimum. He gently touched the side of the wall and invited me to sit down and take it for a test drive.

"Todavía, no" (Not yet), I said, hoping that the word *yet* would convey my enthusiasm for using it when I had a need. Later I found out that others in the group only had a hole in the ground to squat over, and my appreciation for the little outhouse grew.

Rosa showed me to my room, which contained a bare mattress, a small empty table, and a wooden cabinet. It was stuffy but clean, and when she closed the door, I spread out on the bare mattress, relieved to be alone for the first time in over a week. Outside my window, chickens scratched and Bonnie spoke to her daughter in Quechua. Not one word was recognizable to me. A Native language and a mosquito net; it was all so exotic and just as I had imagined it would be when I first heard about Peace Corps ten years earlier. I couldn't help but smile.

Training began the next day, and my fear that I didn't have the skills to help anyone grew. Each week I learned more about the other volunteers who came with me to Bolivia. The training group was a mix of kids who'd just graduated from private colleges, sheltered southern boys leaving their town for the first time, first-generation college students who had worked construction during their summers, and retirees looking for adventure.

"If I can help one person, I will feel like I have succeeded," a girl from New Jersey said when the trainers asked why we were there. Everyone was open to adventure and to new experiences and, most of all, ready to help people. I kept quiet because I didn't know what this group would think about my reasons for joining.

Peace Corps was the best and only option for doing what I wanted to do: see the world, learn some skills, and help people. I sent my application in even though I had doubts about the organization's mission. In college, I heard Noam Chomsky refer to the Peace Corps as the peaceful wing of the State Department. To me, that meant it was more about making the US look good overseas than about bringing real development. But no private business or nonprofit organization working outside the United States could give me the same opportunity for free the way the Peace Corps could. It was the practical choice. My mother's job with the Bureau of Indian Affairs taught me that stable jobs could be complicated. She was often the only Native woman working in an agency that was supposed to be helping Natives.

"It's a good government job," I told my grandmother. Helping people was part of the draw, but I was uncomfortable with the assumption that I knew how to help simply because I had grown up in the United States. It reminded me of the time in college when a white man came into our Native American student center and, without asking for permission, began writing on the chalkboard about the Red Man's mistreatment, as he phrased it. He added an exclamation at the end of his message and smiled smugly, seemingly delighted by his understanding of the problems facing Native communities. Now I was here in Bolivia, wondering if they would see me as I had seen that man.

Jodi, an artist from Georgia, lived with a family a few houses away, and we walked together to the training center each day. She was in my Microenterprise with Youth training program, which meant that our projects would involve working with kids learning vocational skills. Jodi's blonde hair, blue eyes, and charming southern drawl made me initially discount her as a frail flower. She had had a difficult time getting accepted into Peace Corps too.

"That damn recruiter didn't think I could squat in a latrine," she told me one day after we jogged across the crowded highway that we barely survived every day on our way to class. "So I offered to show him how good I could squat." Jodi had a prosthetic leg.

"What would you do if your leg fell in a latrine?" I asked.

"This leg cost $15,000. What do you think I'd do? Jump in after it." We laughed, and she told me about the special foot her doctor gave her so that she could wear sandals.

"Do you worry about what it will be like once you are sent to work somewhere?" I said. I didn't know whether I was the only one concerned about being able to do the work.

"I figure we'll learn it once we get there. Don't worry, you'll be fine." She bubbled with confidence, and I hoped I would feel that certain eventually.

The next week, our training group visited an organization helping homeless children in the city of Cochabamba to see for ourselves what life was like for poor kids in Bolivia. A man named Javier led the tour. With his khaki pants and boots, he looked like any engineer, but his long graying hair wasn't typical of Bolivian men. I knew Bolivia had one of the highest rates of child labor, but

I didn't understand exactly what that meant until I walked through the city with Javier pointing out the children shining shoes on every corner, collecting tickets on buses, working at food stalls in the market, and sweeping the sidewalks outside homes and businesses.

"In the countryside, children tend llamas and goats or work in the mines," Javier continued. I remained silent as always, thinking about the lives these children must lead, how impossible it must be to finish school in these situations. "See those kids huddled under blankets in the park?" He pointed to a group hidden behind a bench.

"They are sniffing glue." He pointed out small discarded plastic containers piled in parking lots. As if on cue, a boy nearby with a dirty sweater cupped a plastic container to his nose and closed his eyes. It was heartbreaking to see, but I didn't know what to do with this information. Addiction, poverty, and the lack of a social safety net were beyond my control. If I were living on the street, I would probably want to be high all the time too.

Why did the story always have to begin with a portrait of poor, suffering creatures who needed help? The tragic story of these kids was uncomfortable and overwhelming, but also familiar. I was reminded of documentaries of Native American reservations that always included images of untended children and Native people lying on the street next to boarded-up stores, heartbreak on top of heartbreak, making it impossible to see the subjects' humanity. These stories held no hope for their subjects and presented them as victims of their addictions or fate or a cruel system that didn't value them. It made them pitiable, powerless creatures.

The layers of dust hanging above the city penetrated everything. A few weeks of constant dust, sweat, and diesel fumes left my clothes dirty, and other than wearing them while I took a shower—an option I considered—I hadn't figured out how to wash them. Bonnie, the mother of the house, said that her teenage daughter would wash my clothes, but I was not going to make Morelia hand-scrub my underwear and socks. That seemed absolutely colonial. I asked to wash my own clothes. The following Sunday, armed with a bar of soap and every last piece of dirty clothing in a stuff sack, I left the house with Rosa and Morelia.

We walked along the wide shoulder of the highway, and I wondered whether there might be some community sink down the road. Heavy buses sped by, honking to advertise the available spots left on board. We took a narrow path between thorny bushes, and although it was still early in the day, the weight and bulk of my bag of clothes made me break into a sweat. When I reached the riverbank, I noticed that there were skirts spread across the tops of bushes, and empty shirts hanging from trees. Women up and down the river squatted over plastic buckets, slapping rolled-up clothes against the rocks, and children not much younger than Rosa splashed in the water, screaming and chasing each other.

Maybe they'd said the word *rio*, but I hadn't thought we'd be washing clothes in the river. I stopped in my tracks, and the girls kept walking forward.

"Señorita?" Morelia's voice rose. My eyes widened. I didn't want to wash my clothes in the river, in any river, but especially not a river running through a city. My life was lived along rivers big and small, and I knew that a stagnant river surrounded by neighborhoods, running under a freeway, had to be polluted. I didn't want to put my clothes into the water. I wanted to run, but knew I couldn't because I had asked for this. There was no turning back.

I stepped over a half-submerged tire near the riverbank and swung my bag of clothes over my shoulder, hoping my hesitation would look like confusion. I did what the girls did and watched as Morelia pulled a pair of her brother's pants out of the bag and pushed them down into the water. It was hard work. In high school, I washed my little sister's clothes at the Speedy Wash every Sunday, but that was nothing compared to this workout. I balled up my sour jeans, squatted down on the bank, and submerged them in the water.

"Is this water safe?" I asked.

"Yes, for washing," Morelia said. I wondered how the other volunteers were getting this household chore done. I heard men bragging about how many times they could wear a pair of underwear before it was officially dirty. Soiled, stinky clothes were all part of the adventure. I assumed that those men would happily pay a girl to wash their clothes when the time came. From the road, this might appear as a quaint scene, like something on a postcard with the caption "Native village women washing their clothes in the river." But down here on my wet and dirty knees, it was different because I smelled the sulfur seeping out of the mud and saw the empty plastic bags floating down the river.

I scrubbed my jeans with the block of green soap while flicking off the flies that kept trying to land on my hand. The girls expertly wadded up the fabric and rubbed two sides together. When I did this, my knuckles knocked against each other. The girls tried not to laugh. I gave up on my jeans and tried to remove the dirt from my once-white socks, but thick, dirty rings remained no matter how many times I dunked and scrubbed them.

"Señorita, let me help you with these," Morelia said when she finished her own pile of clothes and started washing a few of mine. I was grateful, but realized that this was exactly what I had wanted to avoid. After an hour on the river, I was ready to leave. Although my clothes weren't clean, I was tired and ready to accept that I couldn't do it myself. I stuffed everything back into the sack, and we carried our load back to the house. The heavy bag of laundry bounced against the back of my legs.

I wondered why they didn't wash their clothes at home where they had running water, but I knew a question like that might sound judgmental. It was another way of saying, "Why don't you do things the way I have always done them?" Maybe washing clothes at the river was an important place for the women to share knowledge and spend time with each other. But sometimes poverty is glossed over and described as "culture" when really it is an adaptation to a lack of resources. Native Americans turned a little bit of flour, lard, salt, water, and oil into frybread, the golden hunk of fried dough available at any powwow in the United States. Now frybread was part of the culture, but it was an example of what people do when they have few options. Out on the edge of the city where Bonnie's house was, they had access to water for only a few hours a day, once or twice a week. The water systems in Cochabamba were leaky and underdeveloped because the government hadn't invested enough in them. Washing clothes in the river was probably not their first choice.

Part of me wanted to show the Bolivians I was just like them and would try to do everything exactly as they did it. I was never going to be the cringing Westerner, whining about something that seemed bizarre or beneath me. Another part of me was embarrassed about washing my clothes at the river because hiding evidence of my poverty, of the differences I knew existed between myself and my wealthier peers, had become second nature to me. In the US, it was OK for us to pull ourselves up out of poverty by our bootstraps, but no one wanted to see actual poverty. How could I "play" at being poor when until very recently, I had been poor? Regardless of my moral confusion, I still had to find a way to wash my clothes.

The next day, I was sitting on a stool in the training center's kitchen, watching Magda, the cook, toasting grains of rice in a large saucepan. She was a short woman with a full, round stomach that didn't shake when she laughed, and curly salt-and-pepper hair cut short. Her kitchen was the heart of the training compound, and everyone from volunteers to teachers to the maintenance man passed through while I sat there. In my early days at the Center, Magda had given me papaya for indigestion when I asked her for help. Now, whenever I had a problem, I went to her.

"I tried to wash my clothes in the river yesterday, and it was a disaster."

Magda winked at me, and I could tell she was holding back a smile. I didn't want to ask her to wash my clothes, but I wasn't sure what to do. She motioned to the groundskeeper, who was chewing on the sugar cane stalks left over from lunch.

"Your wife, she washes clothes, yes?"

"Claro," he said. Magda motioned with her chin toward him. I had to accept that paying someone to do my laundry was my best option right then. We worked out a deal for his wife to wash my clothes. Within a few days, I had a stack of clean, folded clothes, and I was both grateful and uncomfortable. *Diez bolivianos*—the equivalent of two dollars. It was the first time I had paid anyone to do my laundry. How would I explain paying someone to wash my clothes to my grandmother? But I knew she wouldn't want me walking around in dirty socks. We were there to help Bolivians, but it was clear that they had to help us every single day. Bolivians made our food, told us the words to use, washed our clothes, and showed us where to go and how to get there, but all I had to give them in exchange was money. I wondered when or whether that would change.

3
La Clase de Baile — The Dance Lesson

An anthropologist from Texas stepped to the front of the large room that doubled as the cafeteria. She had come to teach us about Indigenous Bolivian culture. Her wrinkled khaki pants and authoritative manner reminded me of every anthropology professor I had known in college. Long red wavy hair framed her round face. She was researching gender roles in Quechua societies.

"There are over thirty different Indigenous groups in Bolivia." I moved up to the front row to hear everything she was saying. The Quechuas, Aymaras, Guarani, Uru, and thirty other tribes occupied every peak and valley of a country that spread across snowy mountain ranges, immense salt flats, tangled jungles, and sweltering savannahs. During the weeks I had been in Cochabamba, I saw enough Native people to know that just as in the United States, the Indigenous people lived in the cities too. They wore jeans and tennis shoes, drank beer, and watched soccer on TV. They spoke an Indigenous language some of the time or never.

"It is not uncommon for a Quechua man to kidnap his beloved and take her home with him, thus saving her and her family from the shame of having run off with a boy."

"Oh my God," Laura said, "my grandfather in Mexico did that to my grandmother."

Everyone laughed. "I'm serious," she said to me. Presented like this, out of context, the Quechua customs seemed strange and comical, stripped of their significance. Anthropologists often left me feeling like a specimen. In college, there had been a group of anthropology professors who involved themselves with the Native American Student Association. They were earnest but bossy and spoke more than they listened. Yet we needed them to help us navigate the institution's bureaucracy and find funds for a student powwow. Their research and dedication to Indigenous cultures saved sacred tribal sites and helped rescue dying languages. If they deemed something important, it became important. I tried to focus on what this anthropologist had to say, giving her the benefit of the doubt.

"Women in Bolivia have fewer rights and resources than men." Bolivian women were the poorest of the poor, and in a country as poor as Bolivia, that was pretty damn poor. It wasn't the distended-stomach-famine type of poverty we were familiar with that inspired the "We Are the World" video. It was a poverty that required hard choices: school or food, sell your chicken's eggs or eat them, work three jobs or move to another country so you can send money home. Women, and especially Indigenous women, were the hardest hit by this poverty.

Bolivian women also experienced a high rate of getting beat up by their men. Domestic violence was not even illegal in Bolivia. The overwhelming tide of depressing data points about the Native people was horrible. And familiar. It reminded me of the stories told about Native communities in the US. Native women I knew, women in my family, nearly died at the hands of their boyfriends.

I shifted in my seat and looked around the room to see whether anyone was reacting to what she was saying. The person in front of me whispered something to the blonde sitting next to him, then hid a smirk. A guy next to me drooled as he dozed off. I wanted to elbow him, but knew it was losing game.

"I will not delve into the level of sexual violence Bolivian women experience; there isn't enough time. Just know that it is an epidemic." *Epidemic.* That's what was said about sexual violence and American Indian women. Of everything I had in common with Native Bolivian women, this one hit me hardest because it wasn't a statistic; it was my life. From a babysitter's too-curious teenage son to a family friend with a perverted idea of hide-and-seek, as a child I had been repeatedly poked, prodded, and assaulted. I knew what the weight of a man felt like before I was a woman.

I survived by following the rules, making good grades, and never dating until I was out of high school. But it wasn't just me. By the time I reached college, whenever I met a Native woman, I assumed she'd been raped because it was that common. Almost not worth mentioning. From girls who grew up on the rez to urban Indians to girls who attended residential schools—tragedy was our common denominator. I came to believe that this was part of what it meant to grow up a girl.

The anthropologist moved on to discussing the importance of virility for Quechua men, but I couldn't stop thinking about the Native women. This piling on of tragedy by the anthropologist was not giving the whole picture. It reinforced the idea that Native Bolivian women were creatures deserving pity, one-dimensional and helpless. The context and causes were not discussed. This violence was the legacy of colonization, and I shared the impacts of that legacy in my heart, inside my head, and between my legs, yet I didn't feel pitiful.

What did empowerment and development look like for women who grew up experiencing poverty and violence? How does a woman who knows that her daughter's life will be impacted by poverty and violence work for a better, safer future? Native women in the United States lived this reality and, like Bolivian women, still managed to start businesses, create art, and make a life for themselves. I wanted to discuss the lives of Native Bolivian women as if they mattered—because they did to me. Not focus on all the ways their lives were wrong. The room was warming up and I wanted to take off my sweater, but I could not figure out how to do it without disrupting the meeting and bringing attention to myself. I sat there sweaty and angry.

"Any questions?" the anthropologist asked as she moved her map of Bolivia out of the way. No one, including me, brought anything up.

The question I wanted to ask was, "What about the ingenuity it took to make a living in this dry country or the resilience required to survive when outsiders stole your wealth?" I thought about *chicha*, the sour drink that the Cochabambinos were famous for, and how Quechua people chewed the corn kernels to break them down and begin the fermentation process. *Masticado*. Many people found this custom disgusting, but I thought it was one of the most ingenious uses of human saliva I had heard of. I wanted more stories like that about the Quechuas and Aymaras. What would we do when we realized how inventive and successful Bolivians were? Would we have anything to offer them?

"I will now teach you the most important dance in Bolivia." The anthropologist told us to move all the folding chairs to one side of the room, and hit the play button on a small boom box.

"This is *la cueca*." She unfolded a paper napkin and pinched it on one end as she instructed us to do the same. She motioned for the Spanish instructor standing nearby to be her partner. His nickname was Papa Smurf because of his large nose and guileless grin. He looked alarmed, but didn't hesitate when she offered him a napkin. I faced my partner, a solid but short man from Wyoming, and following the anthropologist's lead, raised my napkin high in the air with one hand like a matador preparing to challenge a bull. She placed her left hand on her hip and raised her chin slightly.

"Start the music." Out of the boom box came the familiar sound of the guitar and *charango* strumming that began most traditional Bolivian songs. She demonstrated the wide swings of the dance, which was often used as part of courtship rituals. Papa Smurf mirrored her movements, stepping left as she moved right. Pulling the napkin tight between her hands in front of her, she batted her eyes at Papa Smurf. It was modest and alluring at the same time, the way they almost touched but didn't, the way their bodies moved together then apart. Still, I could not imagine how this dance might be used by a man to get a woman or a woman to tempt a man.

I laughed at myself as I attempted to watch while mimicking her. It had been an intense afternoon, and I was glad to be up on my feet moving. I stepped on my partner's foot and repeatedly bumped his elbow, but a quick glance around the room confirmed that everyone else was struggling with their dance moves. She played the song again, and by the third time, I was able to mirror my partner's movements and step in rhythm to the music.

When the song finally ended, the other volunteers walked up

to talk with her, but I kept my distance. The afternoon had shown me that I had more in common with Bolivians than I thought. Would that change the way I related to them?

4

Primer Viaje a Kantuta —
First Trip to Kantuta

The large map of Bolivia sat on an easel at the front of the training room. Bolivia was a puzzle piece wedged between five countries in the center of the South American continent. For weeks I had wondered where I would spend my two years of service. Finally, the day came when they were telling me where I was going. My stomach gurgled with excitement but also with fear. Training was ending. I would move to a community expecting me to do something beyond learning their language or awkwardly mimicking their traditional dances. The training director called out names, and each time a volunteer's name and city were announced, an instructor standing near the giant map pushed a red pin into the spot where that person would be working.

My friend Jodi, the charming southern artist, cheered when she found out she was assigned to a project in the heart of Cochabamba, at a center for homeless girls. Laura's name was announced, and her pin was pushed into the very bottom of the map along the border with Argentina. I wasn't supposed to care where she was going, but I hoped we would be near each other. Then another girl was assigned to the same town.

"We can be roomies!" she said to Laura. I crossed my arms in front of me. When the training director said my name, I forced myself to breathe. The instructor pushed a pin into a spot near the center of the map. It was nowhere near Laura's pin.

"Un hogar de niños en Kantuta," said the instructor.

"What's an *hogar*?" I asked.

"Like a home for children without parents," said the instructor.

"Orphanage," the training director said. An orphanage? Were they sending me to a Third World orphanage? Images from late-night television ads came to mind, the ones that used guilt and pity to motivate people to give money. Brown and black faces were usually crying or nonresponsive to the flies gathering around their eyes. What could an orphanage in one of the poorest countries in South America hold besides poverty, evil overseers, and vulnerable children? I thought of Indian residential schools, where students were stripped of everything relevant to their culture, including their hair and their traditional clothes, and punished for using Native languages. I had to trust that my government was not sending me to a small town in the heart of this Indigenous country to distance children from their culture under the guise of helping them.

The following week, I boarded a bus for Kantuta to see for myself what this hogar was. I was replacing an outgoing volunteer and hoped to absorb as much information from her as I could in one weekend. I planned to write down every word she said and create a manual for myself. If there were rules to follow, I would survive. That's how I made it out of poverty, to college, and into Peace Corps.

I found the bus with the words *Flota Kantuta* on the side in faded gold paint and knew I was in the right place. A chubby young man sitting behind a table in an empty storefront handed me a slip of paper that was my bus ticket. Sitting on the sidewalk, I watched taxis speed by, narrowly missing each other, and the smell of gasoline and rubber from the tire shops lining the road was overwhelming. A woman in a pollera skirt threw a long braid over her shoulder as she yelled "Be careful" at a skinny teenager loading a bulky burlap bag onto the top of the bus.

The doors opened, and I followed men in battered black fedoras up the steep stairs onto the stuffy but clean bus. The seats were covered in faded blue fabric fraying at the edges. Men and women boarded the bus; some eyed me as they passed, but most did not. They looked like any of the Bolivians I'd met during my time in the country, but because they were from Kantuta, I knew they might become more than random strangers. I looked forward to the day when I could catch this bus and know most of the people.

The bus grunted as it pulled away from the curb, and the tall apartment buildings of Cochabamba gave way to fields and tiny adobe houses. A patchwork of brown and green plots stretched across each valley and up into the hills. The noisy engine pulled us up endless switchbacks and then down, across bridges over chocolate milk rivers that ran through valleys. Steep ledges dropped straight down away from the narrow dirt road. Sometimes the blackened hulk of a long-burned-out bus sat crumpled at the bottom of a drop-off. I smelled the brakes and was grateful they were still working.

A truck heading the other direction came toward us, and my stomach tingled when we moved to the extreme outer edge of the road to pass. The road looked too narrow for one giant vehicle, let alone two side by side. The other passengers chatted while I covered my eyes. How sad it would be if I died on the way to Kantuta, how my mother would cry over an empty coffin while my body remained in the twisted wreckage at the bottom of the mountain. But we squeezed by. Twice more we passed trucks heading the opposite direction, and I stopped looking out the window.

The bus passed over a small bridge, and as everyone pulled down their bags from the overhead rack, I realized we had reached Kantuta. Being taller than most of the people on the bus, I could look over the heads of the waiting crowd. Employees handed down the lumpy packages tied to the top, and little kids tugged on adults amid the sounds of Spanish and Quechua. I wanted to ask someone where I could find Nina, but thought it best to wait until the chaos subsided.

"Hi, are you from Peeze Corp?" asked a skinny young Bolivian man in English as he reached out his hand. He did not launch into the traditional handshake–hug–cheek kiss greeting.

"I'm a friend of Nina's," he said. Nina was the volunteer I was supposed to be visiting, and I was relieved that someone was there to greet me, but unsure of who he was. It was evening in a strange town, and I had nothing to go on but my instincts. Should I trust this man? We both reached for my backpack, but I grabbed it first. In the light of the street lamp, I saw a crooked smile spread across his face, and in that instant, I made the decision to accept his assistance. I had few other choices.

His name was Emilio, and he led me to the small hotel and restaurant his parents ran. Inside the empty restaurant, *Los Simpsons* was playing on a tiny TV in the corner. Once I was alone in my small but clean room, I collapsed on the bed. Then it occurred to me that I was in Kantuta. This was the place where my Peace Corps adventure would happen. I wanted to spring out of my room and bounce down the center of the street like an exuberant Tigger. Maybe here I would find that connection I had hoped for when I arrived, and the Bolivians would recognize I was different from the other volunteers they had seen before.

The next morning while I sipped barely warm coffee and ate a hunk of bread, Emilio walked in with a petite woman with dark eyes and straight black hair.

"La Nina," Emilio announced. Later I found out that she was Salvadoran American. She was weeks away from finishing her service. I jumped up to shake her hand. A former financial manager from Southern California, she had written a grant to fund a workshop where the kids at the hogar would learn to make musical instruments. She didn't smile or ask me how my trip was. Maybe I didn't impress her.

As we walked up the street toward the hogar, every person who passed us on the street greeted Nina. She nodded at each, but didn't stop to talk. I looked forward to the day when everyone would know me, and I would be a part of the town. Emilio pointed out buildings as we walked. The market, the post office, the most reliable foosball tables; he knew where everything was. He leaned in close and whispered in Nina's ear as she pushed him away softly. I wondered if they were a couple.

Three blocks later, she stopped in front of an open metal gate through which black-haired kids wearing white smocks streamed out. A small white church sat just inside, its large wood doors closed. We walked under a sign that read *Centro Infantil* (Children's

Center). The kids watched us pass as Nina led me to a small kitchen near the cafeteria. She introduced me to the cook, doña Florencia, a smiling, rotund woman; Ximena, the cook's helper, who was a beautiful teenage girl wearing the pollera skirt; and a teacher named Teresa with round cheeks and curly hair. I repeated their names in my head, but with no point of reference, I forgot them almost immediately. This was my first opportunity to demonstrate that I knew to shake their hand with my right hand, hug them with my left arm, and kiss their cheek. I had practiced this maneuver in training and managed to get through it without elbowing anyone.

"De dónde vienes?" asked doña Florencia. Her thick biceps and shoulders looked capable of lifting boiling pots of soup and moving them across the room. "Where do you come from?" she was asking me. Not what did I do or whom did I work for, but where was I from.

"Oregon," I said.

"Orejón?" a teenage girl putting away dishes nearby asked. Everyone chuckled. I was confused but wanted to be in on the joke, so I laughed too. The teenager placed her hands by her ears and asked, "Orejona?" Had I said the wrong thing? Or maybe I said the right thing the wrong way. I searched my brain for that word. La oreja meant ear, so orejona must have meant someone with big ears. Here I was coming in trying to look like an expert, and they found something to tease me about. I signed and laughed. I raised my hands to my ears and danced around like a drunk elephant. They laughed. At least they had a sense of humor.

Ximena, the cholita who was the cook's helper, handed me a fresh piece of soft bread as we left the kitchen. I tucked it under my arm as I shook her hand.

"Very nice to meet you," I said with such enthusiasm that I

almost spit on her. Although her name was Ximena, from that moment forward she became Xime*nita*, the diminutive flourish *ita* added to demonstrate extra care and affection. I practiced her name to remember how to pronounce it.

The director of the Center introduced himself, then walked me around the buildings. In addition to the kitchen, there was a large open-air dining hall with long rows of tables and chairs. Unlike at the day-care center where I worked during college, there was no sign of any toys, puzzles, or art supplies, but it wasn't the dark little boarding school I feared when I first found out I was coming here. A little girl missing her two front teeth grinned as she walked by, pulling her long, straight hair up into a ponytail. She looked healthy and not wanting for anything except maybe a new pair of shoes. I wondered what I could possibly contribute to this place.

At lunch, Nina disappeared into the kitchen, and I sat down next to Teresa, the curly-haired teacher, and her table of kids. The girls had long black braided hair, with dark polyester skirts and cotton T-shirts peeking out from under their clean white school smocks. The boys had short, neat hair; collared shirts; and pressed pants. Teresa told me that half the kids attended classes in the morning and the other half attended in the afternoon. They looked at me with timid smiles as we ate noodle soup. The broth was good and salty. A hunk of meat floated at the top of my soup, and I tried to take a bite, carefully avoiding the fat. The kids around me ate everything in their bowl, even cracking open the bones and sucking out the marrow. I wanted to show them I wasn't a squeamish gringa and ate as much as I could. They smiled and looked at each other, but said nothing.

A girl introduced herself as Marisol. She was petite and serious. While most of the other kids only eyed me silently, Marisol told me she was in the third grade and wanted me to teach her English. Of course, I agreed. She took my plate and Teresa's, scrambling off to the sink to wash them before going to class.

All of these shy, averted eyes reminded me of what I was like as a little girl. Sitting across from them at the clean but scratched table, I had to admit that this Center was a good spot for me. I hadn't wanted to come here because I thought I'd be babysitting while my friends would be developing export businesses for farmers or building sanitation projects. But the years I had worked at my college day-care center taught me how to respect and care for children. I could do this.

"Is there another volunteer here? Do you ever see him?" I asked Nina as we left the Children's Center and walked back toward my hotel.

"Daniel? He's gone right now." She continued, "And he had a message for you." She turned to face me as we reached my hotel. "He said that it's a bad idea for volunteers in the same town to hook up." I took a step back. Was this her message to me, or his message? I didn't understand what was going on. Nina barely spoke to me, treating me as an inconvenience, while this dude I had never met was already pushing me away as though he were some one-night stand who thought I was too clingy. I wondered how Laura was doing on the other side of the country and couldn't wait to commiserate with her when we returned.

"Well, I prefer Bolivian men anyway, so I don't think that will be a problem," I said with more fake bravado than I knew I had in me. Bolivian men did interest me, and I had spent a few hours with my lips locked to a handsome engineer at a dance club a few nights earlier, but I was trying to sound like the type of woman who knew what she wanted and went after it. In reality, I was just a pudgy lady trying to keep from being the worst volunteer that ever existed.

"Not me; I don't date Bolivians," she said with a blank expression. Right then Emilio rode up on a bicycle and stopped at the curb in front of us. His wide-eyed expression reminded me of a puppy waiting for a treat. Nina sat down on the handlebars, balancing her petite frame in what looked like a practiced move. For the first time all day, a smile crossed her face.

"Ciao," Emilio yelled as he pedaled away down the bumpy street. It sure looked like they were more than friends. I hoped she'd return a little bit nicer after a few hours spent with Emilio, because I was not enjoying my time in Kantuta with Nina so far.

The next day, Nina decided we were going to visit some people from the States she knew outside of town. I really wanted to learn more about what she did at the Center, but she was the guide for this tour, so I followed her. She, Emilio, and I squeezed into two seats of a truck. During the ride, I asked Nina questions about her work at the Children's Center and whether she had any suggestions.

"I helped them with the books, you know, the accounting. I'm an accountant." She spoke in the past tense as if she had already distanced herself from the Center and Kantuta.

"What about the workshop, the one you got the grant for where they make musical instruments? What am I supposed to do with that?"

"I don't know, sell them. How hard can that be?" she said. Her responses were shattering the little bit of confidence I had, so I stopped asking questions.

The truck left us outside the tall, thick gates of a Catholic mission school. Nina explained that the mission had volunteers from the United States. I wondered whether they were missionaries converting "Indians" to Catholicism. A short, dark-skinned nun in a habit let us in. The outside of the building had recently been painted with fresh white paint and looked newer than the buildings at the children's home. A tall guy with long hair gave Nina a hug.

"Where are you from?" asked a woman wearing a faded Ramones T-shirt. Her dark brown hair and athletic frame made me see her as a prettier, skinnier, Catholic version of me.

"California, but went to college in Oregon." I told her.

"Get out! I used to live in Portland," she said and slapped my shoulder lightly. We found out that a few years back we had been at some of the same demonstrations against old-growth logging held in downtown Portland. It completely upended my assumptions about them when I discovered that these Catholic missionaries were hippies. I had expected straitlaced white men in suits out here passing judgment on Indigenous people. If I'd known them better, I would have asked what they thought about their work. Anyone who'd read one book about the Catholic Church in Latin America knew there existed a long, dark history. Did these cool kids ponder their place in that history as they sat across from Quechua kids teaching them to speak Spanish? I wanted someone to help guide me through the complicated experience I was having, but knew that this quick trip was not the moment to discuss it.

To return to Kantuta, Nina flagged down a truck and asked, in perfect Spanish, whether the driver was going our way. There was no room in the cab, so we climbed up onto the back, which was open.

I moved slowly up the ladder because I could not see what was in the back and imagined everything from pigs to peanuts. From the top, I saw thin green sticks, ten feet long, that looked like bamboo, filling the entire truck bed. Crawling on my hands and knees and gripping onto each stick with white knuckles, I made it to a pocket of space and decided to stop moving because this pickup-stick situation was never going to be comfortable. This was not ideal, but I was relieved to know we were headed back to town.

Nina and Emilio sat toward the front of the truck bed, and the driver yelled something to them. They laughed, and the truck started moving forward. They didn't tell me what he said or let me in on the joke. I was confused and whimpered pathetically, which, luckily, could not be heard over the sound of the truck engine revving up. The mission school disappeared into a dust cloud behind the truck.

We bounced along the rough road, and the steep green valley surrounded by tall hills seemed to narrow. From my perch, I could see the small adobe houses scattered across the landscape, the occasional tree providing shade to a home and everything surrounding it. Cattle standing behind fences made of brush and stacked wood poles chewed their dinner and ignored us. A thin old man walked slowly along the road behind a big-bellied donkey. Neither the man nor the animal acknowledged the truck. Smiling kids on the side of the road waved and yelled as we drove by. My eyes watered from the dust, and I shut them tight every few minutes for an extra second of relief.

I thought about the last two days and the people I had met. It hadn't been the trip I dreamed of, but it had been exciting. *I am riding in the back of a truck through fuckin' Bolivia! This is awesome.* Emilio and Nina were leaning against each other, looking out toward the mountains. How great that must have been to find a Bolivian to connect with, someone to help her on this adventure.

Emilio turned and handed me a small piece of one of the green sticks we were sitting on. They were both chewing on them. Looking at the stick in the fading light, I realized it was sugar cane. Sucking on a stick from the back of a truck in Bolivia was probably not a great idea. But there was no way I was going to turn this down for fear of unclean microbes. I pressed it to my lips and started to suck. At first, it tasted like wood, but slowly a sweet flavor emerged, and the more the wood softened, the more intense was the sweetness. Emilio gave me a thumbs-up and turned back to Nina. I sucked on that stupid piece of sugar cane for as long as I could stand and then dropped it over the side of the truck.

It was almost dark by the time I noticed the houses getting closer to each other and the streetlights on the side of the road as we approached Kantuta. My mouth started to water, and my gut tightened. I knew what was coming next and leaned out the back of the truck. My weak stomach didn't like this aspect of the trip. As I held my hair, I thought: *I am puking out the back of a truck in fuckin' Bolivia.* I wondered if my physical weakness looked like proof that I was unprepared for being a volunteer.

Maybe Nina said good-bye; maybe I thanked her. I don't remember clearly because I was in pain, and it took all of my energy to get back to my small room, where I stayed for two days puking into whatever bucket Emilio could find for me. When I was well enough for the bus ride to Cochabamba, I curled up in a seat and slept the whole trip. Nina was gone by the time I moved to Kantuta to begin my work, and I never saw her again.

5
En la Noche — In the Evening

Two weeks before training ended, I turned twenty-six. Laura asked where I wanted to celebrate, and I chose Tio Lujo's current site. We weren't sure where Tio Lujo's Bar would be from one weekend to the next. It moved to different spots throughout Cochabamba every few weeks. But the Westerners and expats in town always managed to find it. Information about each new location was spread between rooms at the cheap hostels and restaurants recommended by the travel guidebook everyone carried. *Tio*, which means uncle, ran the bar and was from Argentina, Chile, or one of those other South American countries that didn't seem part of the Third World. His black-rimmed glasses were thick and would have looked ironic in the United States, but in a country where few people could afford glasses, there was no irony. The bar had small tables lit by candles, Spanish music playing on tinny speakers, and a menu of food that was familiar but not very tasty. I never found out why the bar moved around, but suspected it was poor management due to too much Bolivian Marching Powder. Bolivia was full of people from around the world who came specifically for the high-quality, cheap cocaine. *Lujo* means luxurious, and no matter what building the bar ended up in, the beers were always more expensive than anywhere else in the city. The bar probably had some other official name, but we called it Tio Lujo.

From the cab we took to Tio Lujo's, we could see the streets filling up with people walking to the Festival of Urkupiña. Devotees of the Virgin Mary made the pilgrimage on foot to the mountain where she had appeared. It was still winter in the Southern Hemisphere, and the pilgrims wore layers of jackets and scarves.

The first round of beers arrived at the table. I hoped someone would bring up the film we all watched during training that afternoon. *Blood of the Condor*, or *Yawar Mallku*, was a 1969 Bolivian film about Quechua villagers and an agency called the Progress Corps. Before starting the film, the training director said, "This movie changed the history of the Peace Corps in Bolivia." All twenty-six of us sat in the large meeting room, which smelled of rice and meat because it was also the lunchroom. We were two weeks from our swearing in—the moment when we held up our hands and promised to represent the United States as Peace Corps volunteers.

The black-and-white film opened with a Bolivian couple in a small earthen-walled room. The wife was young, had smooth skin, and wore a serious expression, but the husband was weathered, and slurred his words. They argued about the death of their children, and the husband blamed the wife for not having another baby. Every word they spoke was in Quechua. I had never seen an entire film in an Indigenous language, and I perked up every time I heard a word I recognized—*warmi* (woman) and *wawa* (baby).

Then the volunteers from the US showed up. Their Spanish

was laughable and barely understandable. One woman wore Jackie O sunglasses and pedal pushers. We laughed. Nervously. Those ridiculous people were supposed to be us. I looked around the room. A woman nearby squinted at the screen.

"We, of the Progress Corps, have come here through many sacrifices of our own so that you can develop," the head of the group said to a line of silent, staring village residents. He was a barrel-chested man wearing the same button-up flannel shirt in every scene. He puffed on a pipe as he spoke with controlled condescension to the Bolivians. Boxes of donated clothes were offered to the villagers, who reluctantly accepted the gifts. I thought of the US soldiers who gave blankets infected with smallpox to Native people, and wondered if the filmmaker was saying something about poisoned gifts. Some of the people in the room were paying attention, but more than a few had dozed off. *Are they seeing what I am seeing?* Maybe this was my paranoid Native imagination.

The line about the sacrifices the volunteers were making for the betterment of the Bolivians sounded a little too familiar. No one had stated it so plainly, because our "sacrifice" for the sake of the Bolivians was assumed. Peace Corps volunteers were the most noble motherfuckers on the planet, or so we were told. The more that personal comforts were forgone, the further away we were from a city, from electricity, from toilets and running water, the more valuable was our sacrifice. That sentiment was as true thirty years earlier when the film was made as it was that afternoon in the cafeteria.

In the movie, the women in the village were never able to get pregnant again after visiting the clinic run by the Progress Corps. The film ended when the villagers discovered that the volunteers were "sowing death in the bellies" of the women of the community.

It was an allusion to the forced sterilization of the Indigenous women. The North Americans were pulled away into the darkness by the villagers, never to be seen again.

"Remember, this was not based on a real incident," the training director said as he switched off the television. He explained that the movie was shown widely throughout Bolivia in 1970, and it wasn't seen as fiction. Peace Corps was asked to leave the country by the Bolivian government partly because of the reaction to the movie. Twenty years later, the organization returned, thanks to a government that was friendlier to the United States.

"Do they really think Peace Corps did…did this to women?! Is that how they see us?" a woman in the front row asked, her brow crinkled in confusion. Forced sterilization seemed beyond her comprehension. The training director assured us that it never happened and that Peace Corps never operated clinics.

While watching the film, I thought about my mother getting her tubes tied the year I was in fourth grade. I didn't know the term *tubal ligation* at the time, but that's what it was. Her baby-making days were over. She wanted me to know she was choosing it. The afternoon my mother went into the hospital, I stood on the playground imagining giant tubes like multicolored hoses snaking out of her, while a white doctor struggled to tie them together. A few months later, she enrolled in community college.

I was surprised that the other volunteers didn't seem to know that forced sterilization was an actual practice. It wasn't just a perfect metaphor for the genocide Indigenous people had experienced but an actual crime committed on Native women up until the 1970s. In North America, one in four Native women were forcibly sterilized. Full-blooded women were targeted first.

Although I knew that the Peace Corps had never sterilized

women, I wasn't surprised that Bolivians were suspicious of the organization's actions. In a world where Indigenous people had been taken advantage of by foreigners and every few decades a new generation showed up promising to help, of course they wouldn't trust volunteers from the US. But I didn't say anything. That evening as I changed my clothes to get ready for my birthday celebration, I wondered what the other trainees would have thought if I'd said I understood why the Bolivians believed the film to be true. Would they see me as unsophisticated and backward? I knew no one would bring up the film on this night of celebration with a handful of days between us and the beginning of our service.

From the inside of the bar, I saw that the number of people in the street walking to Urkupiña had doubled in the short time I had been sitting drinking my beer. Laura sat in the seat next to me, and someone said, "Happy Birthday." I thought about bringing up the movie, but what kind of party would it be if I talked about something as horrible as forced sterilization? Laura and I huddled in a corner with a bottle of wine. My time in Kantuta had been demoralizing, but she had had a blast during her visit to southern Bolivia. She had already put a deposit on an apartment. I drank my wine and hoped that I didn't look as dejected as I felt. The bar filled up with volunteers in town for trainings who had heard about the party. I knew it wasn't really for me, but I loved that my party was becoming a big event.

"Hello, who is that?" a woman behind me said, and I looked up to see a scruffy guy with a battered leather hat walk in. It was

Daniel, the volunteer from Kantuta who had warned me to stay away. With yellow hair, blue eyes, and dimples, he looked every inch the Southern California surfer dude that he was. I assumed he had no idea who I was, and hoped I wouldn't have to speak to him.

"This must be the birthday girl," he said and wrapped me in a hug. He knew who I was and that I was moving to Kantuta. He had heard about me puking out the back of the sugar cane truck, thanks to Nina. I smiled and tried to think of a witty response, but he disappeared back into the crowd. Laura and I laughed as he stepped away and I was handed a shot glass full of Bolivia's finest *singani*.

At some point I had had too many drinks and knew I needed to leave the building. I didn't want to cry on Laura's shoulder and tell her how much I was going to miss her. Saying no was difficult for me, but I knew I had passed my limit, so I sneaked out the door. I did this anytime I was too drunk to pretend that I was having a good time. Sometimes I needed to be alone. I peeked behind me and was both relieved and heartbroken that no one was coming to save me.

Stumbling out into the street, I bumped into a woman who was heading to Urkupiña. It was nearly midnight, but the wide main boulevard was now full of people. Dogs hiding behind fences barked. Many of the people were carrying toy cars, fake money, and tiny houses. Earlier that night, a taxicab driver told us they were replicas of what the people wanted. When festivalgoers arrived at the hill where the image of la Virgen had appeared, a *yatiri* would bless the replicas, and the people would leave them in hopes of having their specific request filled. The mixture of Indigenous ceremony and Christian icons made me think of the prayer said before powwows I'd attended, thanking Jesus, the Creator, and all our ancestors. I wished I had something a yatiri could bless. What could I place on the hill that would help me be the opposite of the smug volunteers in the movie? The three months of training that was about to end had improved my Spanish, taught me a little bit of Quechua, and burned into my mind the shape of Bolivia on a map. But I had no clue as to whether I could help Bolivians. No trinket represented the knowledge I thought I lacked or the experience I hoped to have in Kantuta.

6

El Centro Infantil — The Children's Center

Finally, I was back in Kantuta for good. For $25 a month, I rented a room with a line of windows looking down onto the street. I was a goldfish in an aquarium. The wood floors creaked when I crossed the room, and my new mattress fit perfectly into the bulky green mosquito net. The week before coming to Kantuta, Jodi and I ran through the market in Cochabamba to buy the household appliances we thought we would need. We bought the same multi-speed blender, and she found a large pressure cooker, one of the must-have items according to current volunteers. Instead, I picked out a compact white Brazilian typewriter with my remaining money, anticipating the satisfaction that would come from loudly pounding out my thoughts on my Bolivian experience. I didn't have a table yet, but like everything else I wanted, I was certain it would eventually come. My apartment was a few houses down the street from the Children's Center, and I could hear the dinner bell every night.

On my first day, I arrived at the front gates to find that the kids were already there, ripping off hunks of bread, running to class at the school across the street. They were a blur of white school smocks, skinny legs, and dusty sandal-shod feet. I took a deep breath and knocked on Director Simon's office.

"Ah, señorita, welcome," he greeted me. Simon was from Oruro, in the northern part of the country, and I couldn't always understand what he said because he threw in the occasional Aymara word. He walked me to the cafeteria, and we passed a group of boys pulling wet combs through their short hair, getting ready for their classes. A teenage girl stood on the patio next to a plastic basin of water and used her fingers to create a long, smooth ponytail in a younger girl's hair. A boy who looked to be about ten years old buttoned up the front of his smock.

Simon introduced me to two brothers, Tomas and Umberto, who had recently come to the Center together. Seven-year-old Umberto looked at me without a smile. Tomas, five, flashed a gap-toothed grin. Tomas's pants were too big, and Umberto's shirt was faded, probably from too many washings. I wanted to get down on my knees and hug them both. Instead, I shook their little hands and bit my lip to hide my smile. Umberto pulled Tomas to the cafeteria for breakfast. The director explained that the boys didn't have any nearby relatives and rarely saw their grandmother, who lived in a distant state. Tomas was a few months past his fifth birthday and officially too young to be admitted to the Center, but because everyone wanted to keep the brothers together, they were both let in.

I arrived in Kantuta thinking that every child at the Center had a heartbreaking story of poverty and abandonment. Vulnerable children always scared me because I had once been a vulnerable child and knew they weren't safe in this world. I did not want to be at an orphanage. But by the end of that first week, I realized that these were just kids, some poorer than others and many lucky to be there. Many of the children were from families in Kantuta who weren't destitute but wanted their children to benefit from the meals and supplies they received. Then there were the children whose families lived and worked far out in the rural communities surrounding Kantuta. In the tiny villages where they came from, there were no schools, or the rural schools only went up to fifth grade.

Sunday was market day, when buyers and sellers from the neighboring communities came into Kantuta for weekly supplies. Everyone congregated in the open market building where the cement floor and metal roof protected the sellers and their products from the weather. During one of my first trips to the market, I ran into Joaquin, a quiet boy with a big smile, who was shopping with his mother, a tall cholita with a loose ponytail and apple cheeks who reminded me of my auntie. She pointed to a pile of tomatoes that were plumper than the tomatoes I almost bought. I smiled and nodded in gratitude. She had come to town to shop and visit with him. As Joaquin and his mother walked away, I saw two chubby cheeks peeking over the back of the colorful *aguayo* cloth tied around her shoulders. She was carrying a baby in there. Joaquin turned and gently patted the baby's head. Before that moment, I had only seen him as a shy kid from the Center, not as someone's child or someone's big brother. This mother was sacrificing time with her child, years of their lives spent apart, so that he could get an education and have opportunities she never did. My twenty-six months without a refrigerator seemed ridiculously easy by comparison.

Even though it was Sunday, the post office was open. Kantuta's mailman intimidated me, but there was no other way to check for mail than to face him. He brought to mind a plus-size Vincent Price and made me wonder what the Spanish word was for *stoic*. He handed me a package from my auntie containing no letter but six blank books for writing. It was surprising and perfect. I hadn't confided in her or anyone that I wanted to write about my time in Bolivia, although I had already almost filled the blank journal I had brought with me from the States. My auntie was one of those people with a skill for picking gifts that filled a need I didn't know I had. There was also a letter from Laura. Her project was going great, but southern Bolivia was hot and humid. On the last page, she asked what happened to me at the end of training. She was confused because I had been opinionated and strong when we met— lecturing everyone about colonialism and Indigenous people. But I had acted insecure and conflicted in the final weeks of training. She told me that this experience was hard and that we needed to support each other. She wasn't wrong. I lost confidence every day I was in training. On one of the last days in La Paz, I emerged from our shared hotel room wearing the exact same alpaca sweater and black leggings as she. Hung over and sad, I don't know if I was consciously copying her or on autopilot. It was an extreme example of how I survived by doing what the successful people were doing. I cringed when I thought about it. I loved her for her honesty and hoped that the next time I saw her I wouldn't be so lost.

There was a solar eclipse a few weeks later, and, thanks to the Peace Corps, I had one pair of eclipse glasses. Little Tomas grabbed my hand and pulled me into the courtyard where the kids had cut up cardboard boxes to safely watch the moon move in front of the sun. As the sky darkened, the teachers instructed them to look at the shadows and not at the sun itself. Umberto watched me as I handed my glasses to his little brother. The serious look on his face told me he was trying to figure out whether his little brother was safe with me. Tomas beamed and handed the eclipse glasses to Umberto. I understood Umberto's hesitation because I was more like him— distrustful and reserved. It made Tomas's exuberance stand out. I was glad that Tomas had Umberto, but I was also glad that Umberto had Tomas.

7

La Ch'alla — The Christening

Renaldo, my regional supervisor, came by for a surprise visit. He was charming and warm, with a salt-and-pepper beard and a neatly pressed shirt that made him the picture-perfect example of a Bolivian engineer. He invited me to attend the christening of several water projects. Two water wells and water catchment ponds were finally ready for use after years of work. The opportunity to go out to the countryside for the day was a welcome relief from trying to figure out how to make myself useful—a daily goal I rarely accomplished. I squeezed in between a volunteer named Greg and an official from the La Paz office. The sky was cloudless, the air was dry, and I knew the day would be warm.

In the front passenger seat sat Daniel. We hadn't spoken beyond that moment at my birthday party. I saw him walking through Kantuta in the early evening, dust flying off of his jeans, and imagined that he spent his days in the fields with the farmers discussing techniques for improving yield. I was envious of the experience he was having, or that I imagined he was having.

Renaldo drove slowly over the cobblestones leading to the main street. It was a strange privilege to be riding in a private vehicle, something I hadn't done in over a month. Even sitting shoulder to shoulder in a row of seats was a luxury that gave me the opportunity to watch the people. Women and children walked along the sidewalks toward the market carrying empty shopping bags. The heavy doors of the post office were shut as usual, and I hoped there would be letters from home coming soon. A skinny dog sniffed a discarded plastic bag. The fat man who sold *coca* sat in the doorway of his store behind three-foot-high plastic bags of the green leaves. Daniel waved as we passed, and the coca seller tipped his head in our direction.

We crossed the dry riverbed, and the car sped up as the road widened. The valley opened up to the right of the road, where green fields were spotted with occasional small red and brown houses. A man leading a trio of donkeys tied together stepped off the road as we approached. We came around a bend, and green hills covered with short leafy shrubs came into view. Dirt paths led up and over the hills. The children from the Center followed those paths back to their families in the countryside on weekends.

Greg, the other volunteer, tightened his smile as the vehicle bounced over the uneven road. He had been sick for two weeks, and I was surprised he was there. Diarrhea took out more volunteers temporarily or permanently than homesickness or poorly matched volunteer assignments. I had suffered too, but my body adjusted. I understood the pain, though. Being sick in this unfamiliar country was demoralizing. Lying on a lumpy mattress, drinking warm bottled water, and taking ten trips a day to a latrine intensified the discomfort. I wondered whether Greg was thinking about leaving Bolivia.

"Did Peace Corps pay for these wells?" I asked Renaldo, speaking loudly to make sure he heard me over the engine.

"The farmers are the ones who built these wells and the reservoirs." Daniel answered, not turning his head. "The grant, the pump, that was easy compared to the amount of work the community put in." Each family benefiting from these projects had to commit to over a month of labor to help complete the project. How much work did that take? How many meetings and trips out to their farms to convince them this was worth it? All of it in Spanish, then translated into Quechua, then back into Spanish. This was the first Peace Corps project I had heard of that sounded like real development.

After twenty minutes, Daniel instructed Renaldo to turn off onto a smaller road that led into the fields. Greg groaned as we slammed into a deep pothole. Cholitas in short skirts walked next to men wearing button-up shirts. The farther we went, the more people were walking. My heart sped up.

"We're here!" Daniel yelled as the road ended. Renaldo parked in front of a small mud-and-straw home with a red-tile roof. Daniel was already out of the car. Rows of undulating dirt fields spread out in front of me. Small clusters of trees dotted the landscape between the fields and small adobe homes. The wind blew slightly, stirring up the dust. I was glad I wore brown shoes that day.

Twenty-five farmers, cholitas, and a few small children walked toward the open field beyond the building. The sky was cloudless, and my head was already starting to heat up. The women next to me spoke to each other in Quechua. The men tucked stiff coca leaves into their cheeks and passed around the small green bag of leaves so everyone had enough. The wind blew off the field into the crowd. I stood on my tiptoes trying to see whether the event was beginning. Dirt was under my feet, in my face, and spreading out before me. I fantasized about escaping to a cool room to sit down with a glass full of ice cubes made from purified water.

"Buenos días," a man wearing a hat that was miraculously not dusty said in Spanish into a squeaky bullhorn before beginning his speech in Quechua.

Another man holding the bullhorn called the event a *ch'alla*. A christening. I repeated the word under my breath. One last speaker blessed the well by lighting incense, pouring chicha onto the ground, and throwing confetti over the hole. These were offerings for Pachamama even though no one said that word. Pachamama was sort of like Mother Earth, but she needed to be fed. Any time the earth was disturbed, the Bolivians provided an offering. It reminded me of the sage twigs that are burned at the beginning of powwows or in a new house. No one ever explained exactly what the burning sage was meant to achieve, but I knew it was less about celebrating an accomplishment and more about moving forward with humility.

"Don Daniel," began one man at the bullhorn. Mr. Daniel. He thanked Daniel for his work. I did not understand every word, but the respect he had for Daniel was obvious. I wanted that.

Switches were flipped, cranks were turned, and everyone turned to look at the spigot on the other side of the field. Nothing happened. A man pulled off his jacket and knelt down by the motor. There was banging, and someone yelled, "Ready!" A motor started, and the water gushed out in a huge stream. Everyone clapped.

The dirt rows darkened with water, and the woman standing next to me stepped aside to let the water flow past her. I sniffed and then, to my complete surprise, started crying. This was just a dumb little water pump project, so why was I emotional? On this day, because of months of work by Daniel and hours of labor by the members of the community, there was a well pumping water in a dry, hot field. The impact of that piece of machinery for these people whom I had spent the morning standing next to wasn't small. The water would help the farmers produce and sell more crops. It might be part of the reason they'd stay in the community instead of traveling south to grow coca plants. My knowledge about how economies and politics worked had hardened me to the meaning of one single act like this. It was difficult not to be cynical. I knew that a small community of farmers producing a few more bushels would not lift the people of Bolivia out of the poverty that five centuries of colonialism and neocolonialism had put in place. But that day, that moment standing in the field, helped me see that one small thing could have value. Economic development had never been so tangible to me. It was under my fingernails and staining my socks.

Every single one of those farmers and their children would live a tough, sparse life. But the water was flowing. It was clear that neither Daniel nor the Peace Corps was the savior here, but they had helped make this project a reality. The water was now halfway across the row. Daniel walked toward Greg and me.

"That was really something," I said to Daniel, probably a little bit too quickly.

"Yeah, that was awesome." Daniel's enthusiasm was genuine. His smile was more relaxed than it had been in the morning. The farmer next to him was carrying a bucket of chicha with a dry gourd cup floating around on top. I accepted the invitation to drink the yellow liquid, which was a little bitter and tasted the way fresh bread smells.

"Gracias, Ingeniero," farmers said to Daniel as they shook his hand. His grin widened as he greeted them. Don Hernan, Don

Moises, Don Xavier. I was impressed that he knew their names.

The crowd dispersed and moved in the direction of the little thatched-roof house. Wood benches lined the walls, and the packed dirt floor was flat and dusty. The mud-and-straw walls were cracked but solid and kept the room cool. A woman handed me a bowl of rice, potatoes, chopped onions, and a single skinny chicken leg on top. I balanced the bowl on my lap and used the big spoon to dig in. I couldn't tell whether I was hungry—my head was buzzing from standing in the sun for an hour. The creamy potatoes and the rice filled me up quickly. Twelve people crowded inside the room while the rest milled around outside.

"Are you ready to go to the next one?" Daniel asked Renaldo.

"There's another one of these?" Greg seemed deflated. He wanted to get back to town.

"Don't worry, you'll be back in town by the afternoon," Renaldo assured Greg as he revved up the Land Rover. We drove to the site of a small reservoir. Another ch'alla, and they sprinkled more confetti in Daniel's and Renaldo's hair. I did not cry this time. Another home, another plate of food. This time it was a soup of quinoa, potatoes, and one grisly gray hunk of meat. I was full and beginning to get sleepy. But I had to eat every bit of food presented. To refuse it would be an insult. At the next stop, I was handed another gourd full of chicha. I was not sure how many more cups I could get down. After the fourth cup, I was beginning to feel the familiar loosening of my joints and tongue.

"I can't eat another bite," I whispered to Daniel.

"You have to either drink or eat," he whispered back as a young woman handed him a bowl brimming with rice and pota- toes. "Inside, eat; outside, drink." I stayed outside and tried to hide from the man carrying the bucket of chicha. I pretended to examine the flower on a bush, trying to not make eye contact. But everyone noticed me, and I was invited to a final cup. All of us in the vehicle had sweaty red faces that told me they were as tired, drunk, and sunbaked as I was.

Daniel hugged me when we stopped in front of his room off the main square. Before disappearing behind a big red door, he told me to come over on Sunday for cocktails. It was such a relief to discover that he wasn't an asshole. I thanked Renaldo for an amazing day. I didn't know what I could do in two years that would compare to those projects, but I knew that before too long, I would have to have something to show for myself.

8

Ropa Sucia — Dirty Laundry

My white socks were darker each week, and my hands more ragged from scrubbing. In the cement sink, I mimicked the Bolivian women, rubbing the fabric together quickly and efficiently the way someone who has been washing clothes by hand since she was young could do. But all I had to show for my efforts were raw knuckles. The white socks gave away my inability to properly wash my clothes by hand.

"How do you get your socks clean?" I asked my friends at the Children's Center a few mornings later. I spent more time with these women than with any other Bolivians. How could a grown woman not know how to wash her own clothes? All of them were responsible for their own clothes plus every one of their children's stained shirts, their brother's greasy pants, and their husband's muddy socks. Standing by the metal stove, stirring the enormous pot of soup that would be lunch, doña Florencia told me I had to beat the socks on the cement.

"Like this," said Ximenita as she took an old towel and slapped it against the counter. It made a loud crack, and everyone in the kitchen laughed. Ximenita turned to me and smiled broadly. She enjoyed teasing me and being the center of attention at the same time. Although she was from the countryside, Ximenita was no shy country girl. In her pollera, form-fitting white blouse, and long black braided hair, she was gorgeous and she knew it. "Hot cholita" was the nickname Daniel had given her.

"What are you going to do when you get married?" Ximenita asked. "How will you keep your husband's clothes clean?" I did not know how to say *Laundromat* in Spanish.

"Machina de lava," I said as I mimed feeding coins into a washing machine. They seemed impressed until I explained that it cost one dollar to wash and one to dry. That was a full day's wages for a day laborer. Ximenita clucked her tongue and shook her head. I thanked them all for the advice. Before I could leave, Ximenita pulled me aside.

"Did you hear about Emilio?" Ximenita whispered in my ear. I had suspected that Emilio had been Nina's boyfriend, and although he helped me during my first visit to Kantuta, I hadn't seen him much since arriving. I hadn't been aware that he was gone.

"Who?" I acted like I didn't remember. Ximenita looked annoyed that I was not interested in her gossip. She stuck her lip out in a pout, and I knew that I would have to ask.

"No, Ximenita, please tell me where Emilio is," I said slowly. She stepped in close.

"Nina is bringing him to the United States to get married," she said low but loud. Ximenita seemed satisfied with the surprise I couldn't hide. Emilio and Nina had dated, but I didn't know they were still together. Now he was flying to the US, and it was big news in this little town. It was also gossipy gold I could tell the other volunteers. When volunteers took Bolivians home to the US, the rest of us prepared our judgments. I didn't say so out loud, but I wondered if these relationships had more to do with opportunity or desperation than with genuine love. Were the Bolivians using the volunteers to get access to a comfortable life back in the United States? Was the volunteer somehow being taken advantage of? Maybe that judgment was why Nina waited almost six months after her service ended to bring Emilio to the United States.

"Good for them," I said. Nina was not my favorite person, but it couldn't have been an easy decision.

The following week, Teresa stopped me as I was walking out the front gate.

"Señorita, I can wash your clothes for you if you'd like." She seemed to be holding her breath. I wondered if this might create a weird dynamic between us.

"Are you sure?" I asked.

"Of course, it will be fine. I do laundry for other people all the time." Her hands flew up in the air as she spoke as though she was pushing aside any complications.

"How much?" I had been in Bolivia long enough to know that a price had to be agreed on up front. If she charged me more than I anticipated, more than I thought was fair, I would pay the price, but our budding friendship might be jeopardized.

"Ten bolivianos," she said. Two dollars. That was a fair price, the same I had paid others to do my laundry.

"Está bien," I said, and we stood there awkwardly. I realized that she was waiting for me to bring her my clothes. When I handed her my dirty bag full of unwashed pants, shirts, and underwear, I suddenly felt weird about the situation. Was I taking advantage of her, or was she taking advantage of me? Why were these always my only two options? Teresa was as a single mother; ten Bolivianos would help her support her son. But that wasn't it. This wasn't charity. I needed her help, and I was using my resources to get it. Why was this so difficult?

Four days after handing her my laundry, Teresa and her five-year-old son dropped off my neatly folded clothes. I added three Bolivianos to the total to help me cover up the weirdness I felt. This was privilege in action, but I needed clean socks.

Teresa invited me into her classroom a few days later and asked me to help with the kids struggling to learn English. In between classes, we talked about our lives. In addition to being a single mother raising her own son, Teresa also helped her widowed mother raise Teresa's five brothers. Her dream was to be a beautician, and although she had attended beauty school, the reality of raising her son and brothers did not allow her to do what she wanted. Teresa was the same age as I. She never said this, but I knew Teresa's earnings did not go into her own pocket. Whatever she earned, as well as what her brothers earned, went to the family. I complained about making only $200 per month as a volunteer, but not only was I making more than she or any other person on the staff of the Center, my money was completely my own. I could blow it on a new stereo or a trip or a typewriter.

"Would you help me make bread next week?" she asked me one day as she dropped off my clean laundry. Everyone made bread at the Center; the other counselors had their wives or husbands to help, but Teresa always made hers alone. The possibility of being able to contribute something and support Teresa thrilled me. I said yes instantly because I actually knew how to make bread. The years making sourdough rolls with my grandfather in his cluttered San Francisco kitchen while he patiently explained yeast and the proper way to knead dough were finally going to be useful.

Simon, the director of the Children's Center, was supposed to be helping me, but it was Teresa and Ximenita who became my real guides. I turned to them when I didn't understand something about Kantuta or the Center. They were always patient when explaining things to me. There was a boy in town that Ximenita liked, and she spent hours telling me how smart and sweet he was. She always asked me whether Daniel was my boyfriend because, like most people in town, she thought we were together. She never believed me when I told her we were just friends. But it felt familiar and comforting to sit with a girl and talk about love and boys.

Walking past the one restaurant in town I frequented, I was shocked to find a Dutch woman I had met the previous week in Cochabamba.

"Hello, Blanca, do you remember me?" I reintroduced myself. Maybe her Dutch name wasn't Blanca, but that's what everyone called her because of her white spiky hair. She volunteered at the Children's Center in Cochabamba. She was on her way to Potosí to see the Salar De Uyuni, the world's biggest salt flat and one of Bolivia's major tourist destinations.

"You probably already know Lucas," she said, and motioned toward a thin man with short brown hair sitting across from her. I had seen him walking around, but had assumed he was a tourist.

"No, I do not know you," he said. He laughed. I laughed. He was an agronomist working for an organization a few blocks from the Children's Center. He had been in town for a month. I told him all about what I was doing at the Center, and he said he wanted to buy a charango. I was about to respond when Blanca cleared her throat. I had forgotten she was sitting there. Soon after, he stood up to leave and gave me a traditional but forceful Bolivian hug-handshake-kiss. I wondered if he practiced doing it as I had.

"We should hang out some time," I said, hoping it didn't sound too flirty.

"Mucho gusto conocerte," he said. I watched him walk away.

"You can chase him down the street if you want. I won't mind," Blanca said when he was a few blocks away. I wanted to say, "Damn right I'll chase him down," but instead laughed with a pained smile that I hoped expressed my annoyance. Daniel was out in the countryside most of the time, and, as much as I loved my friends from the Center, it would be nice to have someone else to speak English with every once in a while. I left Blanca soon after and headed home, wondering how long I should wait to visit Lucas.

The following Thursday, Teresa and the girls in her group laughed and gossiped with me as we mixed the flour, lard, and water together in giant bowls. While the yeast worked in the dough, we sat on old chairs in the shade, and the girls asked me questions.

How many brother and sisters did I have? One sister.

Was my mother sad that I was not at home to help her? Probably a little.

Then it was my turn. I asked each of the girls how far they

lived from Kantuta. Most were from communities an hour or more away by foot. What did they want to do when they finished school? Work. College and a career were far in the future, and most did not know what their options were beyond being a mother, working on a farm, or being a teacher. These girls were already more educated than both their parents, but that education came at a cost, and they were expected to help their families financially once school was completed.

I had heard so many depressing statistics about the situation of Bolivian women: high poverty rates, low education levels, and limited access to basic health care. And for girls like these, Indigenous girls from the countryside, the numbers were worse. Yet it was impossible to pity them. They were curious, smart, and funny. Part of me wanted to encourage them to go to college and remake their world. But that was a version of empowerment I learned from a white woman in college, and I found it to be a flawed vision. It was as if everything about Native women's lives was wrong, as if there was one version of liberation—the one preferred by white Western women. Education often came at a cost that was cultural as well as financial. It required sacrifices. In college I never invited the women from my women's studies classes to our student pow-wow because I worried about what they would think of the clearly differentiated roles of women and men at the drums or on the dance floor. The gender roles in my own culture might look backward and unfair to outsiders. And even though I knew there was inequality between men and women in Native culture—I had seen it and lived it—I couldn't walk away because it was imperfect. I had survived by cutting my life up into segments, but that was not the advice I wanted to give these girls.

The dough rose. Each roll was now a perfect little bulging

circle. Finally, we were ready for the boys to lift the large sheets covered with risen rolls and slide them into the oven. Teresa had a firm but calm voice with the kids, never yelling. She was able to get them to behave with a tilt of her head and sideways glance. I hoped she would ask me to help her again next week.

Sooner than I expected, Teresa said my laundry was done. I asked her whether I could come to her house and pick it up after work. I often walked around the streets of Kantuta in the evenings with nowhere to go. I didn't know where Lucas lived, so I couldn't drop by his house. Visiting Teresa would be like having a real friend.

"If it's OK, I'll bring it to you," she said.

"But I want to meet your family."

She pursed her lips together. "Ursula, my house isn't like yours," she said.

"What do you mean? That it isn't a mess and dust everywhere?" Never a good housekeeper, my cleaning skills completely failed me in Bolivia.

"My house is simple. We don't even have a bathroom," she said.

"I don't care," I told her. "I am not rich. I lived in a house with an outhouse." As soon as I said this I realized how meaningless it sounded. She was worried about what I might think of where she lived. A home can give away secrets about you that could otherwise be hidden through wit and style. It is why I never had birthday parties at my house when I was growing up. I dropped the subject. That's what I would have wanted if the situation was reversed. I accepted my clothes and paid her. If she let me come over, I knew I would be the first person from the United States ever to enter her house.

Lucas found me at the Children's Center and invited me over to his house for dinner. Ximenita gave me a look that told me she was dying to know who he was. I didn't tell her anything, hoping to keep one thing about my life private. That night I discovered that he lived in one of the oldest buildings in town, on the main road, and that I had walked by it almost daily. He had transformed an old Bolivian home into a modern living space using abstract paintings and rustic furniture. In English and Spanish, we discussed economic development theory and ate Dutch chocolate while Brazilian bossa nova played in the background. I felt sophisticated and international sitting in his apartment—as though I were part of some multiethnic, multilingual world. His work with the Kantuta Agricultural Cooperative was completely different from my work at the Children's Center. We were both there to help, but his work was measured and effective. He consulted with a team of Bolivian agronomists about crop yields and water collection.

Of course, I developed a crush on Lucas. Not just a little crush, but a whole imagined idyllic future roaming the globe, doing meaningful economic development work, and raising slightly brown children who would speak three or more languages. It seemed perfect and civilized. Under my breath, I practiced the German I learned in high school because I thought that in this imagined future I'd have opportunities to use it. *Bitte und danke.*

9
La Repostería — The Bakery

My Peace Corps supervisor was coming to visit, and I needed to have something to show her what I was doing. Carmen was her name, and I heard she was waging a personal crusade against useless volunteers. I worried that I hadn't done enough to help the Children's Center, enough to help the community, enough to help the entire country, which I believed was my responsibility to single-handedly develop into a thriving economy. The combination of White Man's Burden and Native Woman's Self-Doubt made it difficult to get much done.

When I had arrived at the Children's Center, I was expected to develop a project, to proactively identify a need the Center had and meet that need. I was never good at being proactive, and, to be honest, proactive people annoyed me. They rolled up their sleeves, tucked their hair behind their ears, and charged forward with grand ideas meant to make everything better. I worried about intervening too much in the Center. The other volunteers seemed as though they'd been born to intervene, unafraid to tell Bolivians what to do and how to do it. Maybe they were bluffing, but I didn't even know how to bluff like that. I needed to figure out something soon, because there were expectations to meet and work plans to turn in.

The day my boss arrived, I was in the Center's kitchen, where I began each day. It was the heart of the whole place. Despite two open windows, the room was often dim. The roar of the propane flames and the clanging of pots kept conversations limited. The kitchen workers fed a hundred kids three meals a day. It was the one place where I knew how to help in a direct, concrete way.

"Chop those carrots," Ximenita ordered as she handed me a knife.

"Help me lift the pot of soup onto the table." The cook motioned for me to step over to the bubbling-hot ten-gallon pot.

"Dry these plates and then stack them over there." Clang, plop, knock. These tasks were satisfying and met my need to be useful.

"Is your boss coming today?" asked Ximenita. She smiled slyly while saying this, and I knew I was being set up for some serious teasing. She knew I was nervous about this visit.

"She's going to fire you, right?" she teased. "What do you do around here, anyway?" she asked. A flirtatious smile spread across her face. Ximenita did this every day. She had a knack for finding my biggest fear and teasing me about it until I wanted to walk away. The women in the kitchen laughed, and I had to smile a little bit to myself even as I tried to pretend I wasn't mad.

When the gleaming white Toyota truck pulled up in front of the building, I knew Carmen had arrived. I greeted her with my now almost-perfect Bolivian handshake and hug. Her olive skin and dark hair told me she had some Indigenous blood, but she was no cholita. Educated in the US, she wore a crisp white shirt and spoke in English with no trace of an accent. Director Simon came out of his office and greeted Carmen with a formal handshake. Her Spanish was flawless and fast.

"Good morning, doña Carmen, what a fine morning," he said and then laughed at something he alone found amusing. I quickly led Carmen away from the director, hoping he wouldn't ask her to fund another workshop or build a dormitory or install a soccer field for the kids. These were all things that he had asked for and that they probably needed, but I had no idea what would be the first step in a big project. From the cluttered, bright classrooms where the students did homework, to the latrines and unfinished shower facilities, to the open expanse of packed dirt and brush that was the backyard, I showed her everything I thought was important. The Center had potential, but I did not know what to do with it.

"What is happening here?" she asked when we walked by the screened-in room with the ovens where Don Lucas and his students were elbow-deep in the bread-making process. Twice a week, students and teachers made bread because it was less expensive than buying bread for one hundred kids. Two skinny teenage boys lugged a full tank of propane gas across the dusty courtyard toward the ovens. Both the boys and the girls helped mix the dough, often competing to see who could make it the fastest. Once the dough had risen, they rolled it out and shaped it into fist-sized balls.

"Come in and help us make the bread," a teacher yelled out as he rolled two white balls of dough with the palms of his hands. The veins on his arms stood out as he quickly threw the balls onto the baking sheet and grabbed two more. He bragged that he could make five hundred pieces of bread in a week. Carmen crossed her arms and surveyed all the activity. I wondered if it would have looked better if I had been making bread when she arrived.

Carmen liked to catch volunteers in the act and a friend told me he had heard that Carmen couldn't contain her excitement when she came upon a volunteer in a remote village who was knee-deep in mud, holding down a pig while trying to vaccinate it.

"What about the charango workshop?" Carmen turned and asked me. I knew she'd want to see the Peace Corps–funded workshop. Earlier I convinced a few kids to be working on their charangos when she arrived. As we entered the building, I heard the sounds of children pounding metal and scraping wood. The workshop was in an open room and had three large wood tables covered with vise grips, sandpaper, and tools I couldn't name. Wood, glue, and sweat were in the air, and lining one wall was a large stack of roughly formed charango bodies that I thought of as guitar fetuses.

By now I knew that charangos were small ten-stringed musical instruments perfect for tucking under an arm and strumming while walking down a dirt road. Nina's grant had paid for all of this as well as for a teacher, Miguel, to mentor the kids and teach them the traditional art of putting the instruments together. Miguel stood over the table, demonstrating how to scrape out the inside of the charango body. He was a stout but strong man with black curly hair and a thick brush of a mustache. Before she asked, he began explaining how to make a charango.

"Como un siki de wawa" (Like a baby's bottom), he said as he rubbed his palm over the back of the instrument, speaking in the mix of Quechua and Spanish that I was only now starting to understand.

"Where are the girls?" Carmen looked around the workshop. "Aren't they learning how to make the charangos too?" "How are you going to market the instruments outside of Kantuta?" Carmen drilled me with questions, and I stumbled for answers. The truth was, I didn't know how to market musical instruments. My degree was in economics. I could make a pretty graph showing the rising value of the dollar against the Mexican peso, but knew nothing about actual business transactions. I didn't consider asking for help. Asking for help would have revealed that I didn't know what I was doing. If they knew how lost I was, they might send me back home.

"The girls are probably not going to make charangos," Carmen told me when we returned to the Center. "You have to find something else for them." We sat in the large open cafeteria next to the kitchen, and I wondered if this was the moment when she was going to tell me I was not doing enough.

"The bread is ready," said Ximenita, in her soft, breathy voice and set down a tray of freshly baked rolls. Her delivery was probably an attempt to help me, and I mouthed "Gracias" as she stepped away. Carmen crunched into the large flat bread roll. The spongy white interior and dark crust were tangy and warm. "Is this from...?" Carmen motioned toward the room with the oven, her mouth too full of bread to finish her question.

"Yeah, it's cool. Every week they make bread," I said. I tried to appear alert, but was exhausted from trying to impersonate what I thought a proactive person looks like. I wondered whether she would leave soon.

"What about a bakery project with the girls?" she said. "Involve the kids, not just in the bakery but in the planning. You need them to take part in every step of the process."

"But every store in town sells bread," I said.

"Then figure out what isn't being sold and make that. Have the kids do the feasibility study." I was not an entrepreneur, but the wheels in my head started turning.

"This isn't about money." She turned and looked me straight

in the eyes. "This is about giving kids skills that will make them successful. Anything you do to help them understand that they have options in life will be worthwhile." Carmen fell silent for a long moment, and I attempted to start a conversation about microlending and the Grameen Bank. I wanted her to have some confidence in me, and I wanted to show her I understood the concepts of development even if I did not personally know how to start a development project. I exhaled with relief as the shiny Toyota finally disappeared down the cobblestone street. I wasn't sure where to start, but knew that I had to show Carmen that I had at least tried.

Simon, the Children's Center director, didn't like the idea of the *repostería* (bakery) and told me there was no disposable income to spend on the supplies. I showed up the next day with a bag of flour. He wasn't convinced. I promised to buy all the supplies.

"Señorita, what you don't understand…," he began, but I couldn't hear his voice over the steam billowing out of my ears. I asked his wife, doña Florencia the cook, if she had any ideas. She shook her head.

Then one day, with no advance warning, he mentioned the bakery during one of his regular morning lectures to the children. "Señorita, please tell us about the project," he said, and every head in the cafeteria turned in my direction. I stood up.

"We'll have our first meeting…next week." It was a decision I made as I was saying the words. Who knew whether I would ever have another chance?

"We'll help you, señorita," four teenage girls who had made

bread with Teresa told me afterward. I didn't know whether they were interested in starting a bakery or simply bored. I didn't care. I was happy to be doing something. The first class was in a dusty classroom crowded with old school desks. We discussed basic concepts about buying and selling. One afternoon, we walked around the market to see what people were selling and how much they were charging. The girls clung to each other and whispered. I asked a woman how much her bread cost.

"Un peso," she said, looking at me with a tired frown. This was at least twice what I usually paid for bread, and I knew she was giving me a special marked-up price because I was a gringa. I could pass for a Bolivian woman in a fitted dress and flats, especially on a busy day or in the city. But here in the town, in my town, I was clearly an outsider. Celia, a tall, quiet girl with a crooked smile, looked at me. They needed to be the ones asking. I stepped back and motioned for Celia and the other girls to do the rest of the research.

A few weeks into the project, the girls discussed what they wanted to bake and sell based on their research. *Rollos*, the sweet turnovers full of jam, were their number-one choice. I looked at their faces and for the first time felt like a real volunteer. This was what I had imagined Peace Corps would be like and how I had pictured myself when I saw brochures full of blonde, freckled girls intently explaining something to African women in headscarves. I wondered if this moment with them would be good for a brochure. Of course, it would be difficult to tell who was saving whom, because their hair was like mine, dark brown, and our skin was the same.

They could be my cousins. One afternoon I asked Celia to take a picture of me and two of the girls sitting in the courtyard. Years later, this picture ended up in my high school reunion slideshow. Everyone told me how cute my daughters were and congratulated me for being a brave single mother.

"Doña Teresa, I need your help," I said as we sat at a long table in the cafeteria and played Chinese checkers the following Friday. "You know I've been working with the girls on a bakery project."

"And?" she said.

"We want to bake next weekend, but we don't have a recipe. The girls want to make something called rollos, and I was thinking…" I trailed off as I realized that there was so much I needed help with.

"You will need sugar, lard, marmalade, eggs, and milk. I'll write it down for you." She jumped her marbles over mine, and I knew she would probably win this game.

"Thank you. I appreciate the help." I didn't only need her recipe; I needed her.

"Who else is helping you with this?" she asked. I told her the names of the girls. She looked at me for a long moment. "What time are you going to be baking?"

"Early Saturday, nine o'clock," I answered.

"Nine?" she said, pausing to move her last marble into place, thus winning the game. "Bueno. You're going to need some help. I can come for a little while, but need to be home before lunch." This was a huge favor she was doing for me.

Teresa came early on that Saturday morning after she had already spent several hours baking pastries at home for her brothers to sell at the market. The rollos we were making were sort of like turnovers with marmalade inside. The one ingredient I couldn't find was *azúcar pulverizado*—powdered sugar. Teresa poured a cup of granulated sugar onto the surface of a flat rock, then rolled a rock back and forth over the sugar until all of the granules were pulverized under the heavy stone. A pile of white powdered sugar was all that was left.

"Azúcar pulverizado," she declared as she stood up and brushed off her hands. I was amazed. I thought of every time I had carelessly sprinkled powdered sugar on the table or thrown away a bag that was almost empty. I thought of the unconscious choices a person with wealth makes, the assumptions about what was easy and available. Like my middle school basketball coach, who instructed every player to buy a second pair of shoes for basketball without realizing that my mom could afford only one pair of new shoes. As much as I wanted to charge ahead with this project, I knew I needed to have Teresa and the girls participate in planning, to avoid unnecessary sacrifices my choices would entail.

Within a couple of hours, we had several dozen rollos. We giggled as we ate the few that had turned out funny looking. The room was sweltering from all the baking. The inkling of accomplishment energized me. We sold half that afternoon and the remaining the next morning. I meticulously kept track of who sold what and how much money they would get at the end of the day, because the whole point was to teach them that by working they could get something in return.

Teresa finally invited me over to her house after that first weekend with the bakery. I met her mother, who wore a pollera, had long gray braids, and laughed at her own jokes. The three of us spent a Saturday afternoon drinking chicha on their patio while they told me stories about living in Kantuta before it had electricity. Teresa's three younger brothers came in and introduced themselves while we sat there. They had recently graduated high school and worked around town. Like Teresa, they spoke Quechua with their mother but Spanish with me and each other. I noticed Teresa watching them as they spoke to me. I wondered if she had briefed them about my visit. Sitting there with them was relaxing, and I was happy not to feel the pressure of trying to help anyone.

Teresa and her family were Catholics, like most Kantutans. But the Children's Center was run and supported by an Evangelical Christian organization, and all of the other staff were Evangelicals. Even though the staff members were friendly with Teresa, I always sensed a slight tension between her and the other teachers. I thought it was because she was the only single mother on the staff and, as the child of a single mother myself, I knew that people thought they had a right to judge a woman's life. Now I saw that it was bigger than that. Like me, she was struggling to fit in at the Center. For the first time, I realized that she and I could support each other.

After several weekends spent working with the girls and gaining momentum for the bakery, I went to Cochabamba for a party with other volunteers. I spend the day enjoying the anonymity of the big city and bought sugary treats that I never could find in Kantuta. Before catching a cab to the party, I went to the large telephone office and called my mother. Standing in the clear Plexiglas stall, pressing the receiver into my ear, I told her about the success of my project. I felt like a real volunteer, and I wanted to tell someone.

The party was in one of the crash pads volunteers shared in the city. Most volunteers worked in the countryside, but for many, sharing an apartment in the city was more convenient and cheaper than any hotel. I had never considered getting one, then found out that for five dollars a month, I could have a spot on a couch for the three or four days a month I was in the city. Even I could afford five dollars. The party that night was at a place on the edge of town near the lake and was full of people I did not know.

"You're Ursula, right?" asked a tall Latino guy from Montana who was returning to the States in a few weeks. "How's it going at your site?"

"Great, but sometimes I think it is the Bolivians who are helping me." I explained my project and the help Bolivians had given me every step of the way. The beers loosened my tongue, and I decided to be honest with him.

"Peace Corps lets us know ourselves at our lowest depths," he said. People didn't usually talk about the dark side of the experience. He gave me a hug that I didn't realize I needed. I immediately developed a crush on him. Then a beautiful Bolivian woman walked up and put her arm around him.

"Conoces Arianna, sí?" he introduced his fiancée. In that moment, I remembered that I had met her a few months earlier. I needed to be more careful with my crushes. Besides being gorgeous, she was genuinely warm, which was probably good for him.

I was glad to have an answer whenever people asked me what I was working on, and to listen to them describe their projects. I was able to hear their struggles without thinking that everyone was doing more than I. The spirit of celebration made me accept a few too many glasses of whiskey, and then someone handed me a pipe with a nugget of pot. Thinking I was invincible and forgetting my low tolerance for weed, I inhaled deeply. But my capacity for whiskey mixed with other substances was low, and before long I wandered outside and passed out in a field next to the house.

In the first hours of the morning, I stood up and saw that my ankles were covered in red welts from some biting insect. Ants? Mosquitoes? I had no idea. Why hadn't anyone come to get me? I lumbered back to the house, where I found a floor crowded with curled-up bodies, the room smelling like whiskey, stale cigarette smoke, and bong water. The danger of passing out in a field alarmed me. I drank quite a bit, especially during training, but had never passed out on the ground in a neighborhood I didn't know. I missed Kantuta. It was where I wanted to be now, not here. I drank in Kantuta, sometimes to excess, but I always made it back to my house. What would Ximenita think if I passed out in the street? *Qué barbaridad!* I could imagine her saying it now. I caught the bus to Kantuta the next day, happy to be heading back to a town that was starting to feel, not exactly like home, but at least like a safe place.

10

Misiñawi — Cat Eyes

Strikes across the country shut down the schools for weeks, and the children from the Center went home. The teachers' union was not satisfied with the small raise the government had promised teachers. Most teachers I knew made less than half the $200 monthly stipend I received. But teachers weren't the only ones protesting; factory workers, coca farmers, and others who opposed the government of the US-supported president Gonzalo Sanchez de Lozada were also involved. Roadblocks of trees and rocks were used to create literal stoppages of food and fuel to pressure the government to meet protesters' demands. Because Bolivia had so few roads, blockages of selective roads could bring everything to a crashing halt. Protests like this were common because Bolivians, especially Indigenous Bolivians, had few elected officials representing them. The teachers in Kantuta marched through the streets at night with candles. I saw my landlord's wife, but wasn't sure whether it was appropriate to wave at her from the sidelines as though it were an Independence Day parade down Main Street.

I was still able to buy food and supplies at the market, but didn't attempt to travel to Cochabamba for fear of getting stuck on the wrong side of the blockades. Both the charango workshop and the bakery project sat idle, but every day I still walked up to the Center because I knew my friends would be there, and I had nothing else to do.

"Sabes que? Estoy pensando en dejar mi pollera." Ximenita said one morning as we all snacked on the last of the bread. I dipped it in my coffee, softening the edges a little. I didn't understand what she meant by *dejar mi pollera* (leave my skirt), and looked at her.

"Dejar, quitar?" She said it a different way, but I still didn't get it. I understood that the words meant to leave, to quit, but still was confused.

"Ah, Ursula, don't you understand?" Teresa asked. "She doesn't want to be a cholita anymore." Ximenita didn't want to wear the traditional Quechua dress anymore.

"Why would you want to do that, and what would you wear?" I knew there were fewer Bolivian women wearing polleras than in previous decades, but I didn't think this was how it happened—one day a woman decides to stop being a cholita. Ximenita explained how expensive the pollera was and how much money she'd save if she could dress in regular skirts and dresses. Teresa and Florencia nodded their heads in agreement. Both women were children of pollera-wearing cholitas, but they didn't wear traditional clothes. It had to be about more than money.

"And everyone says that cholitas are from the countryside and thinks that they are *Indios*," Ximenita said. *Cholita* was synonymous with *Indian*.

Bolivians told me all the time that they were proud of their

Incan ancestors, and the kids often bragged that *Kantuta* meant Sacred Flower of the Incas in Quechua. Yet they knew what many people, especially the wealthier, whiter population of Bolivia, thought about *los Indios*. Few wanted to be seen as an Indian. For a young woman like Ximenita, living in town for the first time in her life without family nearby, being seen as a cholita made it that much harder for her to succeed. Maybe she didn't want to be a cook's helper for the rest of her life.

"What do you think I should do?" Ximenita looked straight at me. All I could think was, *This is not right.* The choice she faced symbolized why cultures disappear, why languages get lost, why my grandmother told my mother not to braid her hair in high school because it made her look too Indian. I thought Ximenita should stay a cholita, but it wasn't my place to say. It was easy for me to think my friend should wear a pollera when I didn't have to walk through the world as a cholita. And I understood why she wanted to tuck away her Indigenous identity, despite being proud of it, in order to survive. Maybe she wouldn't put it in those terms, but that's what seemed to be happening. The feminist in me wanted her to be able to do whatever she wanted.

"You know, I'm an Indian, like you," I said. They all laughed.

"You're not an Indian. Maybe a little *Indígena*, but not an Indian." Teresa said. I was a bit crushed by this comment, seeing as connecting with Native people was my reason for being there. When I asked them what the word *Indio* meant to them, they described loincloth-clad savages who lived in the jungles along the border with Brazil.

"And you probably shouldn't tell anyone about being Indian; people can't tell by looking at you," Florencia suggested. Whether they wore a pollera or not, I knew all three of these women were

Indigenous. They spoke Quechua, could prepare traditional foods such as *uchuku*, and held ch'allas and other ceremonies that the people from this part of the Andes had been practicing for centuries. Even their aversion to the use of the word *Indio* was similar to Native people in North America. *Indian* was the old word, a word my grandmother used, but only within the family. In my Native American Student Association group, we called ourselves Native or American Indian more often than Indian.

I kissed Ximenita's cheek as I stepped out, and told her I loved her no matter how she dressed. The next time I saw her she was wearing a new sleek, tapered skirt and T-shirt. Her hair was no longer braided and instead rippled down her back in dark streaks. She was as lovely as ever, and I told her so. This had been her choice to make, but I hated that the world made her choose.

The strikes apparently wouldn't be ending anytime soon, and doña Florencia told me that she had decided to visit her mother in the countryside. When she asked me whether I wanted to come along, I jumped up and immediately said yes. Except for the well christening in the country with Daniel, I hadn't spent any time with people in the countryside. I imagined the time in *el campo* would be idyllic and relaxing; the stars easy to see, the sunsets uninhibited, the air fresh. The day-to-day struggles of my work were grinding me down. Buzzing with anticipation, I packed my sleeping bag, a portable water purifier, and a roll of Bolivia's best single-ply purple toilet paper. I rolled up my travel mosquito net and stuffed it into my big backpack. When I met up with doña Florencia, her teenage daughter Lena, and her two younger boys the next day, the wide grins on the kids' faces made me think they were as excited to take me to their grandma's house as I was to accompany them.

Doña Florencia was not a poor woman. Her husband was the director of the Children's Center, and she was the cook, but we did not even discuss the possibility of paying someone to take us to her mother's farm. We were walking. She and her children carried bulging woven plastic bags full of mangos, tomatoes, and bread for her mother. I wore thick-soled leather boots with microfiber socks to wick away moisture. Doña Florencia and her children wore flip-flops.

"It's not far," she said when I asked how long of a walk it was. She motioned with her chin and pointed with her lips to the horizon. "Just over there." Nothing but more of the rolling dry hills that surrounded Kantuta on all sides.

We followed the wide, unpaved road leading east out of town. I followed behind the children as we walked along in single file. The car horns, clucking chickens, and barking dogs of Kantuta faded with each step and were replaced by the sound of the wind stirring the eucalyptus trees lining the dry riverbank. The red clay tiles on the houses on the horizon stood out next to the brown and green of the landscape. I followed the oldest boy down a steep embankment and across a wide, almost-dry riverbed. I realized we were now well out of Kantuta. There were no houses or fences or roads as far as I could see, only rolling hills and the same dry scrub wildness stretching in all directions. I had no idea where we were. In the small stream flowing weakly at the bottom of the riverbed, a half-submerged plastic bag bobbed on the surface. "Just over there" had a different meaning for me than for doña Florencia. For her, it was a place you could arrive after a day of walking.

As we walked, the children asked me about my family back home in the United States. They were surprised to hear that I only had one sister. Doña Florencia told me about her big family. Did she say she had six or seven siblings? I often confused the two numbers. *Seis, siete*. Doña Florencia had walked this road to and from Kantuta every day as a child to attend school. I couldn't imagine a child crossing this distance daily. It reminded me of my own grandmother's stories about going to school with her sister in the mountains of California. They would sing songs and clap their hands as they walked, hoping to scare away the rattlesnakes that hid under rocks. Long walks through snowy winters and rainy spring months made them strong as it must have made doña Florencia strong.

A short truck hauling people and cargo passed us. The trucks were not semis like the ones I was accustomed to seeing in the United States but had smaller, more compact front cabs and beds open to the air. They added passengers or extra cargo for a fee on their route. As this truck passed, I could see the tops of men's hats swaying in the back, their hands grasping the metal bar running down the center of the bed to steady themselves. One dollar. That was probably the cost to carry all of us to our destination. I considered offering to pay for all of us, but hesitated. Using my money to make my life easier was what I had been doing since arriving. The gruff engine pulled the truck up the switchbacks, and clouds of dust drifted in front of us. I jumped onto the side of the road. Dodging cacti and hopping onto barrel-sized boulders, I tried to get away from the dust.

We reached the top of a small hill, and a wide valley opened up below us. Brown thatched roofs were all I could see of the homes on the edges of fields. Doña Florencia and the children kept walking. They had probably passed this spot hundreds of times.

After two hours of walking, we turned onto a narrow road thick with green bushes on both sides. The older children sped up and disappeared. We came upon four small buildings and an open courtyard. We had arrived. Her mother's house was empty except for us. I was relieved to slide the backpack off my sweaty back.

It was like every Bolivian house, a compound of rooms around a central open courtyard. The rooms were in various states of completion. Some had no doors; some had no roof. Were these in the process of being built when the family ran out of money? The kitchen had a roof but no door. Little white flecks of straw that had been mixed with mud speckled the adobe walls. Other walls were painted white and led to rooms with beds or stacks of burlap bags. This home had no electricity, no running water. And no bathroom. No latrine or even a hole in the ground covered by a board. Thank God I had brought my own toilet paper. This family, like all Bolivians in rural areas, went for a walk into the countryside when they had to go.

An older woman in a black pollera and shirt walked into the courtyard. Doña Florencia's mother, doña Manuela, greeted me with a polite handshake and a kiss on the cheek. The musty smell of goats surrounded her. She was probably in her early sixties, but her gaunt face had deep crevices and was dark as leather. Her cloudy eyes showed the first evidence of cataracts. Two long gray braids hung down from her head, and she wore a black felt hat with a few twigs and dry, curled leaves from her day in the countryside.

"Imaynan kashanki?" (How are you?), I greeted her. It was one of the few Quechua phrases I remembered. One corner of doña Manuela's mouth seemed to rise slightly. She said something back to me in Quechua.

"Mana intindinichu" (I do not understand) was all I could

come up with. She said something in Quechua, and everyone laughed. Doña Florencia explained that her mother said I looked like a cat because of my green eyes.

"Misiñawi," the mother said again. Cat eyes. I repeated it, and this time she smiled. My hazel eyes took on a green tint when I wore green, as I was that afternoon. I liked this word *misiñawi*. It was sweet. My light eyes gave away my mixed-blood heritage and were the lasting markers of the Spanish and Irish men in my lineage. Most Bolivians had brown eyes, and light eyes were seen as attractive.

Several strips of raw beef hung from a wire stretching the length of the courtyard, drying in the sun. *Charki*. Dried meat. I was a fan of beef jerky and dried salmon, so maybe I'd like it. As I watched a hundred flies walk all over the meat, I felt squeamish about eating it. I joined the women in the tiny kitchen and tried to help prepare dinner. Soup with noodles and vegetables boiled in a charcoal-black pot that sat above the flames. The smell of smoke filled every corner of the little kitchen, and I had to step out. The mother filled large ceramic bowls with the steaming soup. As the guest, I was given my food first. I was more tired than hungry, but the greasy broth tasted good after the day's long walk. I discovered a small piece of charki under a potato. The impossibly chewy texture reminded me an old shoe. I tried not to think of the flies I had seen earlier. I was a guest and was not going to refuse food they were serving on my first night.

We ate as the sky turned from light to pink to dark. This was the countryside I had been hoping to see, the remote retreat without clocks or honking horns. Staring at the flames, we communicated in a telephone game of Spanish to Quechua to Spanish. I understood about half of what was said. Occasionally, I heard the fluttering of wings and wondered whether there were owls or maybe other birds looking for a place to rest. What must it have been like for Florencia to grow up here? How much work awaited her once she completed the almost two-hour hike from Kantuta after her half day of classes? Girls were expected to work. This I understood. Every girl in my family cooked and cleaned to support mothers who worked. My chores were easy compared to those of the Bolivian women, and even though dishwashers and microwaves sped some things up, we were still folding clothes, making beds, and chopping onions no matter where we lived.

Once the sky was completely dark and the fire was dying down, I pulled out my bright one-person tent covered in netting. Holding a tiny flashlight in my mouth, I unrolled the tent, opened up the poles, and was pleased to find that I had an instant bug-proof room. I was too tired to brush my teeth. There was a specific type of exhaustion that came when I spent the day speaking Spanish. The work it took to understand what everyone was saying and then to communicate a coherent response in Spanish—for hours—drained me. Underneath my sleeping pad the courtyard was hard, but I was happy to be hidden in my little white net. I turned to say goodnight to Florencia and her children. They were sitting on the bed in a nearby room, staring at me, smiling as if they were watching a fascinating nature documentary. When they saw me looking at them, they laughed and did not stop for several minutes.

Even before the rooster announced the new day, doña Manuela was starting the fire in the kitchen. On my cheeks, I felt the cool morning air. Florencia and her mother spoke to each other in Quechua in the kitchen. There were no clouds overhead, and as I watched the moon fade away into the brightening sky, I wondered what the day held. The children walked out of the kitchen carrying steaming cups of something, and I knew it was time to get up. The chipped porcelain mug I was handed was full of purple *api*, a hot corn and sugar drink. I missed my morning cup of instant coffee. Now I wished I had brought some. I sat on a plastic chair on the patio sipping the sweet, thick liquid and realized I had not brought food or any gift to my hosts. This family was sharing their food and home with me. Before I left Kantuta, my primary concern had been with making sure I had whatever I needed to be as comfortable as possible. I knew better. I searched my groggy brain for the Quechua phrase for *thank you*, but came up with nothing.

After breakfast, the kids, both human and goat, guided me on a tour of the hills surrounding the house. I was glad to have my boots as we hiked up steep, dry hills and snaked between thorny bushes that grabbed my pants. The kids found a nest of ants that produce a type of honey and asked me if I wanted to try it. I was here to experience new things, but the thought of sticking a dirty twig into a live ant nest for a slightly sweet goop was more than I wanted on that uncaffeinated morning. I distracted the kids by asking about the rubbery pink and orange bulbs growing out of the top of a nearby cactus. Prickly pear fruit. I had never seen them. Carefully, the kids picked a few and wrapped them in their shirt to ask their mother to prepare later. We came upon rows of brush that were used to herd, then capture wild guinea pigs. I had only been served *qui*—guinea pig—on festival days because it was considered a delicacy. How many times had I looked out of a bus window at this Bolivian landscape and thought it held only clingy thorns, rocks, and insects? But, like the huckleberries on the slopes of Mt. Hood that my mom and I picked, there was abundance in a landscape that looked dry and dead.

When we returned to the house for lunch, I was exhausted and ready to rest. The big bowl of soup I was given had an extra-large piece of charki in it. I thanked them in Spanish for the meal. Doña Florencia smiled a tiny smile, and her mother nodded her head in my direction.

"We're going to make *humintas* this afternoon," Florencia told me. Humintas were sweet little tamales without any filling. I bought them in the market whenever I found them. Doña Manuela pointed to an area behind the house and said something in Quechua. I followed the oldest daughter, who picked up a basket, and we walked into the cornfield. She picked quickly and outpaced me three to one. I wrapped my tender hands around the thick corn, pulling down and out until the tall stalk released the ear to me. In less than an hour we had a basket full of fresh corn.

In the kitchen, Florencia demonstrated peeling the corn husk and scraping the raw kernels off the cob into the waiting bowl. My slow progress was easily outdone by the children and Florencia. When I threw a corn husk onto the kitchen floor, Florencia told me to save the husks and showed me the pile she had quickly accumulated. When the last cob was stripped clean of kernels, Florencia poured the corn onto a flat, two-foot-square stone in the corner of the kitchen. She rolled out a large crescent-shaped rock. This was a *batán*—their food processor. Rocking the stone back and forth quickly with practiced ease, Florencia ground the corn into a thick, lumpy mush. I asked to give it a try, and all three women watched as I awkwardly moved the stone over the corn. Now I understood why every Bolivian woman had arms like a bodybuilder. I could barely move the ten-pound rock.

The humintas were cooked inside the corn husks that I thought were garbage. Florencia's daughter Lena had the hardest job of all, wrapping the slippery green husks into perfect little knots and dropping them into the blackened pot of boiling water. As we sat in this kitchen, mixing the ground corn with spices and lard, Florencia spoke to her mother in Quechua and to Lena in Spanish. Lena understood the Quechua her grandmother spoke, but beyond a few words, preferred to speak Spanish. It reminded me of the times my grandmother went between Karuk and English when we visited older relatives.

In these three generations, I saw cultural assimilation. Manuela was a traditional woman who wore traditional clothes. Her daughter, Florencia, had been a cholita when she was a child. By the time she was in high school, she was wearing the straight polyester skirt and T-shirt that was now her regular outfit. Lena never wore a pollera. Manuela's granddaughter Lena had access to opportunities that her grandmother and even her mother never had. She was already planning on following her older sister to attend the university in the city. This reminded me of the women in my family. My great-grandmother never went to school and spoke almost no English. My grandmother learned English in school, and as a teenager went to Arizona to attend the Phoenix Indian School, but had to drop out before graduating to help her mother. To find work, she moved south to Oakland, California, and spent the rest of her life in the Bay Area. Her sister and brothers remained in the mountains of northern California. The further away my grandmother moved from her family and her culture, the more she assimilated. She had a good job as a cashier at a five-and-dime, but she almost never spoke Karuk and forgot many of the words. Her decision also changed my life; I spoke less Karuk and had less of a connection to the land and the culture than my relatives who never left. It seemed as though that was the price. Education and economic empowerment were available to Lena as they had been to my grandmother, but the only way to achieve them was to leave behind her culture.

Was I part of this family's assimilation? That was not why I joined Peace Corps. I joined because I wanted to help people get out of poverty through economic development. But having to choose between development or culture was a choice someone outside the culture had thought up. A choice that someone who didn't have to leave her culture to thrive would present. Stick 'em up—your culture or your future.

What gave me a shred of hope was the ways that Indigenous cultures, both Manuela's and mine, were not erased. Lena spoke Spanish, understood Quechua, and was as genuinely Indigenous as her pollera-wearing grandmother; just as my city-dwelling grandmother was as Karuk as her sister who remained near their birthplace. The only options for survival forced a person to shed her culture like a restrictive skin that was keeping her from growing. That was the nature of the development forced on Natives in the United States in boarding schools and reservations. As Ximenita's decision to stop wearing traditional clothes demonstrated, Indigenous people faced these choices every day. But could there be another way? Could a country, a community, a person thrive both economically and culturally? As a Native person, I hoped so.

The sweet steam rose from the pot and spread across the kitchen. The humintas had to boil for an hour. Lena and her brothers spent the time talking about their favorite things to eat. I tried to describe a taco and a tortilla, but after an entire day of speaking mostly Spanish and some Quechua, my brain was not firing on all cylinders. Mangoes were the one food we all agreed on.

Doña Manuela finally emerged from the kitchen with a large plate filled with humintas. How satisfying it was to unwrap the hot corn husks to reveal the steaming sweet moistness. It had taken us over three hours to pick, grind, and cook the humintas, but in twenty minutes they were all gone. This was my favorite moment of the weekend. I was thousands of miles from home, but in a dusty courtyard, after an exhausting day, I was connecting with Bolivians over a meal we had created together. Well, sort of together, because, really, they had done most of the work. Once we finished eating, I crawled stiffly into my tiny mosquito net. Even the kids were too tired to tease me.

I knew it was time for me to leave even before opening my eyes the next morning. My scalp was itchy, and my hair was stuck in the shape of the ponytail I had left in overnight. I was ready to go back to my little rented room and stare at the wall for a few hours. Staring at the wall had become one of my favorite ways to relax; it was like watching TV except without the visual stimulation or the constant reminders that my breath stank and that everyone could see my dandruff. After another breakfast of sweet, thick api and bread, I was ready to break the news.

"Are you scared we're going to put you to work again?" asked doña Manuela in Quechua that Lena translated. I laughed lightly, but she had nailed it. I considered myself tough, but I knew that this sixty-year-old woman and her fifteen-year-old granddaughter were infinitely tougher than I was. Doña Florencia told me I should head out to the main road and start looking for a truck if I didn't want to walk all the way back to Kantuta. I had already packed my mosquito net and sleeping bag into my bulging backpack. Doña Manuela stood with her hands on her hips and looked into my eyes. She said something in Quechua I didn't understand.

"Why are you so sad?" Lena translated. Sad? I held my breath so I wouldn't cry. I had been walking around sad and frustrated for months. Being in this country was tough. Trying to start a project at the Center was tough. But I was a strong woman doing my best not to let the sadness and frustration rise to the surface. Why she said this to me at that moment I did not know. I felt exposed. All I knew to do was reach around to hug her.

"Gracias por todo." (Thanks for everything.) And I meant it. But I had to leave at that moment or I'd start sobbing.

The morning birds were still singing as I walked down the dirt road toward Kantuta. I heard voices and quickened my pace until I emerged on the highway. Several women were loading burlap bags onto the back of a truck. The man sitting in the cab was staring off into the distance. I asked if he was headed to Kantuta.

"Seis" was his answer. I handed him crumpled bills, jumped into the back, and waited for the women to finish loading their cargo. We bumped along quickly, and I watched the landscape speed by. Even though the truck was going less than thirty miles an hour, it seemed swift compared to the speed at which we took the road before. The back of the truck was full of dusty farmers heading to the market in Kantuta to sell their crops. It was Saturday, and tomorrow was the big market day. The men stared off absently as they dug into little green bags of coca, popping single leaves into their mouth and pressing them against the inside of their cheek. Dust clouds billowed behind the truck. I held on tightly to the metal bar in the middle, swaying with each turn and hoping to keep my balance. Within thirty minutes, we were crossing the main bridge into town. I slid in front of an old man who smelled like coca leaves, eager to get out of the truck and into my room.

Unlocking the front gate of my house, I wondered what exactly it was that I was doing here, being part of the engine of development changing this country. Development meant a college education for Lena, but it also meant that doña Manuela's granddaughter would lead a different life than Manuela had. As different as my life was from my grandmother's. I filled my teakettle with water and sat staring at the wall, waiting for the whistle that would tell me it was ready for my Nescafé.

11

La Noche Más Fría del Año — The Coldest Night of the Year

"Are you comfortable?" Rowena asked.

"Yes, I'm fine," I answered. We sat facing each other on hard plastic chairs in the empty Children's Center office. A window was open, and a breeze lightly rustled the papers on Rowena's lap. All the dark corners and the bare cement floor made the room dank and not unlike a dungeon. A sagging bookshelf on the wall looked ready to collapse at any time. Rowena's wavy red hair reflected bits of light, and her pale freckled skin reminded me of a breath mint. Rowena was a British college student who had arrived in Kantuta a few days earlier. For her dissertation, she was researching the impacts of economic development on migration patterns.

"Can you tell me about your project and anything you feel is germane to the topic?" She scanned my face as she spoke, stopping at the brown smudge of a birthmark above my top lip. As my skin had darkened from living life outside, my birthmark had become more prominent. Her stare made me uncomfortable, and I stiffened a little. Then her eyes moved back to her paper. Did she really use the word *germane*? I hoped my answers would not sound as stupid as I felt.

"My program is called Micro-Empresas con Jovenes." Her brow crinkled, and I guessed that she did not understand Spanish. "Micro-Enterprise with Youth," I said with one gush of breath. She looked down to her paper and scribbled something.

"Tell me more about what you do on a daily basis."

"I wonder that myself." I waited half a second for a laugh or a smirk that didn't come. Her face remained blank. Clearing my throat, I began with my rehearsed answer: "I market the charangos the boys make in the workshop, and I started a bakery project with the girls to teach them business skills."

"How long was your training? Was it sufficient to prepare you for your position?" She looked straight into my eyes. This felt like an inquisition.

"Three months. Mostly language classes, but also some culture and business training. It prepared me for the basics, but...," I hesitated, not sure how complete an answer she wanted. "But it wasn't until I was on-site, coming here every day, that I understood what was going on and how I could help the Center." She shifted in her seat a little. Outside the room, two of the teenage girls were fixing each other's hair and talking quietly as they prepared for their afternoon classes.

"You called yourself a volunteer, but didn't you say they pay you?"

"Well, only enough for rent and food," I said.

"How much? If you don't mind my asking."

I crossed my arms in front of me. I did mind her asking. Maybe because I had always been poor, I thought that asking how much someone made was rude. I wondered whether there was any way around this question.

"All volunteers receive a living allowance to pay for necessities." She was still looking at me, waiting for an answer. "Two hundred dollars," I finally said. "A month."

"And how much does the average Bolivian make?" she asked. I shrugged my shoulders in fake ignorance. Well-paid teachers made about half what I did, but I was not sure what she meant by "the average Bolivian," because construction workers were lucky to get a dollar a day.

"This is an awful question to ask, but do you think it was worth the money it cost to get you here? The training and the housing and everything?" She pursed her lips and poised her pencil on the paper in front of her.

"I hope so. I mean, I hope I'm worth it to the Bolivians." I asked myself this question daily, but I wasn't about to tell her that. I tried to be useful, but each day I had a small mountain of struggles to contend with—the language and cultural misunderstandings; my lack of knowledge about how the Bolivian economy worked; the challenges of being a young, unmarried woman in a culture where women held little power—all while missing my family and friends on the other side of the planet. This was hard, and I didn't think I was doing a good job. I wasn't about to tell her any of that either. I wanted her to think I had this, that I could handle it.

She finished with some questions about Peace Corps as an organization. I answered them, but that question about my value gnawed at the back of my consciousness. Finally, she thanked me, tucked her pencil into her backpack, and excused herself. I stepped out into the bright sunlight, blinking and wondering whether the US taxpayer money spent to buy my ticket from Miami to La Paz and keep my belly full of quinoa and chewy meat was worth it. If *I* was worth it. In my family, I was considered a success because I graduated from college. I had managed to defy the presumed path for my life and arrive at the ripe old age of twenty-seven without getting knocked up. Here in this world, I felt like an imposter. I had a degree, but no idea what I was doing. When Rowena looked at me, maybe she saw a clueless Westerner, living a life that was luxurious compared to that of most Bolivians, and not doing much to help anyone. Throughout my life, people had passed judgment on me many times, but never had I been thought to have too much privilege.

The next morning, I awoke early and crawled out of bed as fast as I could. It was the eve of the Festival of San Juan, Friday, June 23. I had no idea what to expect for the day ahead. The festival celebrated the life of St. John the Baptist, but was also the winter solstice. According to Bolivians, June 23 was *la noche más fría del año*, the coldest night of the year. The best way to approach the miserably cold night was face first with glasses full of chicha raised high in a toast.

Fridays were my favorite day to be at the Center. It was *día de los deportes*, and the staff and children played games all afternoon. Teresa regularly kicked my ass at Chinese checkers, but after all these months, I was finally learning and ready to challenge her. It was the one day when the weight of helping the Bolivians was lifted from my shoulders. On Fridays, I was simply another staff member of the Children's Center.

After dinner, I went for a walk to see whether there were any bands celebrating the festival. There were fewer trucks and more people than usual on the streets. I watched a man stack several large pieces of wood upright. An older Bolivian woman lit the sticks at the bottom of another stack of logs.

"What is this?" I asked her, motioning toward the sticks.

"Una fogata," she told me. A bonfire. As the flames moved up the sticks, the wood cracked, and white smoke escaped from the pile. *Una fogata.* All day the women at the Children's Center had been saying the word, but I had had no idea what it meant. I stood there watching the fire burn, drawn into the sticks shrinking as the flames surrounded them. With a wave to the woman, I walked on toward the center of town, passing more fogatas being constructed or lit. The smell of burning wood was strong, and I wondered how many fires there were throughout the town. Winding my way past the market and the telephone office, I emerged onto the main street running through Kantuta.

It was busy with cars and people moving in all directions. A man dragging a bulging plastic bag walked toward the night bus to Cochabamba. A group of teenage girls with long black hair clutched each other and walked down the sidewalk like one creature with eight jean-covered legs. Two men strummed charangos and harmonized on a song. The only word I recognized was *palomita*, which meant "little dove."

"Ursula," I heard in a familiar accent. It was Lucas, the Dutch agronomist. I hadn't been looking for him, but now that I found him, I took a step toward him on the curb. He stood next to a Bolivian engineer who was almost always with him. Tall and slightly pudgy, he wore glasses and did not stand fully upright. He was a thinking man in a world that preferred men to be tough, with strong hands. I nodded to the engineer, and he tipped his head slightly in my direction.

"We were eating *la cena* here and then walking." Lucas pulled his hand out of his coat pocket and motioned up the street. "And you, Ursula, where are you going?" I loved the way Lucas pronounced my name, smooth and fast as though he had been saying it his whole life. It almost made up for all the substitute teachers in elementary school who mangled it as if to imply that no one on earth had ever had this name before.

"Nowhere in particular," I said. "Have you seen these bonfires everyone's got on the street?" We turned to look at another fire being lit a block away. The Bolivian engineer mumbled something in Spanish to Lucas and then walked away. I was relieved because I didn't think he liked me. I was happy to have Lucas all to myself.

"I heard about a little willage named San Juan. Just outside of town where everyone goes for tonight. Would you like to walk there with me?" Did he just say *willage*? How adorable. But I did not want to embarrass him, so I kept quiet. More important, this sounded like a date. Maybe? I could never tell. My own insecurities about whether a smart agronomist from the Netherlands could find me anything more than a curiosity, and the three layers of culture—mine, Bolivian, and his—clouded the meaning of every word between us.

"Sure, I'm up for anything," I said. And I was. A unique cultural event in a familiar setting. The familiar and the exotic. In these moments, I knew why I sometimes connected with anthropologists despite my distrust of the profession. I was uncomfortable when those same anthropologists directed their gaze at Native people because we became subjects, not humans. Still, I understood their fascination.

We walked the streets of Kantuta for the next hour. Each time we stopped to speak to anyone, he invited us to drink. "Ingeniero," they called to him. He would share his cigarettes with me and the men who had invited him to drink. The traditional way to spend the night was outside around a fire with friends eating grilled meat and washing it down with chicha. When I first arrived in Bolivia, the festival activities seemed to be just one more disorienting event that disrupted our training schedule. Now I was eager to see how each town celebrated its own festivals in its way.

At 10 p.m., Lucas asked me whether I still wanted to go to San Juan. I was ready if he was. We set out on foot and spent more than an hour walking along the unlit winding gravel road. We did not know how far it was, and several times he stopped and asked whether I wanted to turn back. Despite the chill, the walking kept us warm, and I knew that eventually we'd come upon someone who would help us find the way. What I didn't tell Lucas was how much I enjoyed this moment, out here under the moon, walking and easily sharing stories. Was I imagining it, or did we have something here?

Before too long someone did come along—a teenager I recognized from Kantuta. He was walking back from San Juan and told us exactly how to get there, and soon afterward we saw a large bonfire blazing by the side of the road. A man with a white felt hat sat beside the fire playing a charango. The fire warmed my cheeks, and I relaxed my shoulders. The longer I stood there, the better it felt. A hefty Bolivian with a pile of curly black hair stepped into the circle of people surrounding the fire and nodded to everyone. He was wearing a long red poncho over his slacks and cradled a charango. I recognized him from a meeting at the mayor's office back in Kantuta. He joined the *campesino* in the white hat for a song in Quechua. I understood enough to get that the song was about a woman, *un warmicita*, who had broken his heart. I looked up to the sky. We were miles from any city, and the stars spread across the night sky from horizon to horizon. I peeked at Lucas and was happy to see he had the same grin I did. This was a moment of joy. I felt privileged to stand there, surrounded by Bolivians, in a little village celebrating the coming of winter.

When the man from the mayor's office finished playing and put down his instrument, he was immediately offered a cup of chicha. He refused it at first, saying he was sick, but then reluctantly accepted. This was more than simply a drink. This was generosity and gratitude in a cup. Halfway through a regimen of antibiotics to get rid of the latest version of intestinal parasites, I understood the difficult position he was in when offered a drink. To refuse it was rude, doubly so if a poor person was inviting a wealthier person to drink. It would be like telling him that his generosity was not good enough. The official splashed some chicha from the cup onto the ground for Pachamama and poured the rest down his throat quickly. Handing the empty cup back to the campesino, he nodded and began playing his charango again.

There was nothing more Native than the interaction I'd just witnessed. At times like this, it seemed North American and South American Indians were cousins. That connection between food, generosity, community, and gratitude was so integral to my understanding of the world that I found it difficult to believe that it wasn't universal.

Two gourds full of chicha later, we excused ourselves and headed for the rumble of a truck loading up for Kantuta. Lucas and I jumped into the back. It was nearly 1 a.m. by the time we reached the main street of Kantuta. We stood on the street near Lucas's apartment, and I said good night to him. I did not want it to end. The chicha and the darkness made me bold.

"Will we ever be more than just friends?" I asked as we stood in his doorway. I bit my lip and felt my heart pounding. A bonfire lit up the street a few feet away, and people in ponchos huddled around it, their hands open to the flames.

"No, I do not think so," Lucas said in a crisp accent, his hands tucked into the front pockets of his jeans for warmth. He was not unkind, simply honest. He shrugged his shoulders and leaned forward to kiss my cheek before saying good night.

I walked back to my house, passing bonfires and invitations to drink. I hunched my shoulders against the cold as I stepped carefully on the uneven cobblestone street. Back in my room, I crawled into bed fully clothed. Outside near my window, two men stood around a fire, talking too low to hear. Their mumbling was comforting, and I drifted off to sleep listening to the sound of their voices. I was embarrassed for thinking that I was wanted. I vowed never to let that happen again.

12

Amigos — Friends

The next morning, I stayed in bed as long as possible. I was embarrassed that I had once again misjudged a man. Since arriving in Bolivia, I had only engaged in drunken hookups with other volunteers that never turned into the first night of a relationship that I wanted. Sometimes it was pure lust, meeting my need to touch someone and be touched. But when it wasn't, I never let on that I was interested in finding out whether we could be more.

Looking outside my window, I noticed a steady trickle of people walking to San Juan, taking the same route that Lucas and I had the previous night. Some people forced chairs and bags of food onto buses. The sun shone down through a cloudless sky, and I knew it was going to be a warm winter day. The blackened wood from the previous night's bonfires had been removed or burned up. A curly redhead stood out among the black braids. It took me a moment to realize that it was Rowena. She looked left and right, watching the people around her. I stepped back into the shadows of my room, not wanting to be seen. I worried that she would ask me to be her communicator and guide to San Juan. After last night, I did not feel that I could help anyone. When she disappeared into the market, I decided to head to San Juan to see what it looked like in the daylight. A long walk was what I needed to get me through the day.

"Hola, doña," Teresa said with exaggerated formality as she opened her front door with a towel draped over her shoulder. Before leaving town, I decided to visit with Teresa and see whether she wanted to come to San Juan. She let me into the large room that was the main part of the house. A thin blue curtain hung from a wire on the ceiling, separating the front room from the area where they all slept. I saw several beds behind the curtain and wondered who slept where. Her son sat watching cartoons on a small black-and-white television.

"Hola, doña Teresa." I purposely overannunciated the words, and we both giggled. This was our little game. We liked to pretend that we were discussing important business when usually we were talking about laundry or men. I followed her into the cool darkness of the unfinished room out back where the sink was located.

"How is your Dutch agronomist?" she asked, raising her eyebrows suggestively. Curly black hair framed her round face. Teresa knew all my secrets, including my crushes. She was my best friend in Kantuta and the only person I felt comfortable confiding in.

"I have no idea how Ingeniero Lucas is, and I don't expect to talk to him anytime soon." Teresa looked up from the laundry she was folding. I told her about our evening and the question I asked him at the end of the night. She was surprised I'd asked him directly. This was not something she would say to a man. I assumed she wouldn't ever have to ask it because I'd been told that Bolivian men rarely hid their interest. She frowned when I told her his answer.

"There will be others," she said, touching my shoulder. I was grateful to have Teresa as a friend—a real friend who helped me through the crushes and the rejections. I would like to say that I followed this moment of caring with a question about her life, about her romantic prospects. But I didn't. I was a twenty-seven-year-old woman obsessed with her own life.

"Do you want to walk to San Juan with me?" I asked.

"Maybe tomorrow. I have to finish washing the clothes." She threw a pair of boy's pants into the cement sink.

We said good-bye, and she waved with one hand while turning on the spigot with the other, beginning another sink full of laundry. Teresa told me about a shortcut to San Juan that led from near her house. I was uncertain about taking it until I saw a portly couple step onto the narrow dirt path. I followed them through the low hills outside of town, through the green scrub brush and the occasional cactus. In less than an hour, I came over a low rise and found the village of San Juan. Families were spread out across the hillside.

I sat down on a rock near the top of the hill and watched the community that had gathered. Kids chased each other while grandmothers set out plates of food. The sour smell of chicha mingled with the starchy smell of boiled potatoes. A skinny guy in a dirty shirt played an accordion and sang a sad song about a cholita. I didn't understand the words, but could tell it was sad by the tone of his voice. Beyond the families was the road that Lucas and I had arrived on the previous night. A steady line of faded and scratched buses deposited passengers, then lumbered away for more. I recognized people from Kantuta, but no one I knew well enough to greet. I was the only non-Bolivian on the hillside that afternoon. To me, this was a cultural experience, but to everyone else, this was a reunion, a family get-together at a place that meant something to them. I was an observer, not a participant. It was interesting, but left me cold. After an hour, I walked the long path back to Kantuta.

Days passed, and I kept getting messages that Lucas had stopped by to see me. Maybe he was feeling guilty for his quick rejection. I didn't need his pity. Then one evening he came to my apartment and asked me to join him for dinner. I couldn't think of a good excuse not to go. Over plates of rice, potatoes, and tomatoes, he told me he'd gone back to San Juan a few times with the other engineers and stopped by my house each time on the way out of town to see whether I wanted to come. He asked where I had been.

"Around," I said. "I walked out there the day after…after we were there." He looked me in the eye as if he had no memory of our conversation.

I tried to be a pleasant dinner companion instead of the sullen rejected girl I was. He was being nice. It was annoying. I noticed him watching me silently as the waitress took our orders and while I pulled money from my wallet. Was he studying me? What was he trying to figure out? I hoped he was having second thoughts. That he regretted what he'd said.

Leaving the restaurant, we stepped directly into the path of Rowena.

"Hello, Lucas," she practically screamed, a smile spreading

across her freckled cheeks. Wait—how did she know him? Earlier, she had asked me several times to introduce them. I didn't forget. I did not want to introduce the smartest, whitest woman in town to him for fear that he'd choose her.

"Hello. Oh, do you know each other?" he asked, turning slightly toward me.

"Yes, we've met," I said.

"Are we still on for tomorrow?" she asked him, ignoring me.

"Yes, of course. Come by the office at nine." He turned to me. "Rowena is going to interview the engineers and me about our work." My smile was as weak as I felt. We stood there in silence, looking at each other. Finally, Rowena said good-bye and skipped away. Or at least it looked like skipping. As though she was giddy about this white European connection they shared. I almost rolled my eyes, but decided against it. Lucas invited me to chocolates at his apartment, but I told him I was tired and needed to get to sleep.

"Thanks for inviting me to dinner," I said. He leaned in and kissed my cheek. My arms almost betrayed me by reaching out and hugging him. Instead, I kissed his cheek and said good night.

A week later, I was awoken from a Saturday afternoon nap by someone pounding on my door. I was hiding in my little rented room. I did not want to see anyone. But it was Daniel. A lit cigarette dangled from his chapped pink lips, and his glassy eyes revealed that he had already enjoyed several rounds of chicha. He had been gone for a few weeks on vacation to Brazil.

"How was your trip?" I asked. I never told Daniel about my crush on Lucas. I didn't plan on telling him about what happened while he had been away.

"Words cannot do justice to the amazing time I had." This comment left me confused, but I knew asking again would seem uncool, as though I were an interrogating nerd. "But more important, let's go drankin', honey!" he said.

"Meet you there in a few?" I said. He relented, walking away. I had been living in Kantuta for almost a year, and he knew me well enough to know that I did not want to come out but that I would because he was asking me. Daniel inspired me to take every opportunity to have fun. When Daniel was around, I wanted to stay up all night to see the sunrise, grab the microphone in the kara-oke bar, and eat the wrinkled chicken foot in my soup. To Daniel, life was about the experience. No guru ever had to tell him to Be Here Now because his feet and consciousness were already firmly planted in this exact moment.

Thirty minutes later, an open door, the sound of men laughing, and the acidic smell of fermented corn told me I had found the right place. The *chicharia* had a high ceiling and red wallpaper. Old women hunched around small square tables speaking Quechua. Young men sat on benches along a back wall, and a man wear-ing shiny soccer shorts flung his hands about wildly as he spoke. An engineer scooped out a gourd of chicha from a faded orange bucket and handed me the murky yellow liquid. It was sour, so I drank it down immediately. I submerged the gourd into the cold drink, and Daniel took the dripping scoop from my hand. I still wasn't always comfortable with this charming man who seemed to be succeeding even when he was just sitting there. But I appreci-ated being drawn into his adventures.

After my sixth cup, I was thirsty for that sour taste. I stuffed several dry green coca leaves into the side of my cheek. The musty taste was always a surprise and woke me up a little. In about twenty minutes, I looked like a stoned chipmunk. Daniel disappeared out the door, but I didn't care; I was feeling mellow. A middle-aged woman wearing a faded pollera came over to our side of the room. She eyed me and made a joke about one woman and all those men. It wasn't acceptable for a single woman to go drinking with men. I knew that, but I also knew that I occupied a place of privilege in this town because I was from the United States. I could break rules.

Right then Daniel walked through the door with Lucas.

"Look who I found," he said as he dragged Lucas to our table. Everyone including me stood up and greeted him. Daniel pulled up a table and threw out a small leather dice cup. It was time for *cacho*. I was happy to have a distraction. Cacho was a dice game like Yahtzee. Everyone in Bolivia played it, and it always involved alcohol. Lucas was as nice as ever, asking me how things were going at work and telling me I should stop by for hot chocolate some time. I said yes in that distracted, noncommittal tone I adopted whenever I wanted to say no. He watched me out of the corner of his eye, and I pretended not to notice. Someday we'd be friends again, but not tonight.

Time sped by as we indulged in the Bolivian trifecta of chicha, coca, and cacho. I was never very good at cacho, and my performance worsened as the evening wore on. My cheek bulged with a soggy wad of coca, and I dripped chicha on the front of my shirt. I felt less and less attractive with each round. I was the last person a cultured man would want to be with. But instead of pulling back, I dove deeply into this repulsive version of myself. I accepted all the chicha offered me and asked for more coca leaves. After a round of games that the Bolivian engineer won, Lucas stood up. He mentioned an early morning meeting and said his good-byes. I thought

I might be happy when he left. It only reminded me that I was alone. The energy to stay and drink was gone. Five minutes after he left, I stood up.

"I'm tired, Daniel. I don't think I can do this anymore." Daniel waved me away, and I was immediately forgotten as the remaining cacho players pulled in closer around the table. I heard the dice tumble for the beginning of another game as I left.

Once home, I zipped myself into my mosquito net and pulled the sleeping bag over my head. My mind raced through the men at the chicharia, the rejection from Lucas, the struggle with my job at the Children's Center, the knowledge that it would be a year before I could see my family and friends again. I stewed about all the ways I was disappointed with my life at that moment. I had been in Kantuta for less than a year, and things did not seem to be on an upswing.

"I lost every damn game of cacho," I said. The sound echoed in my empty room. The streetlight outside the window illuminated the layer of dust on the cold wood floor. The stacks of books I wanted to read stood on the rough, unpainted table. My lumpy backpack leaned against the wall with clothes spilling out of it. This room was not a home, more of a temporary resting place. The combination of the alcohol and the coca coursing through my body at that moment caused a dark idea to slink across my consciousness.

Climbing out of the mosquito net, I considered the best options for killing myself. I flipped open my pocketknife and saw the streetlight reflected in the tiny silver blade. Crouching down on my knees, I pressed it against my left wrist. I hesitated for a moment, took a breath and then pulled it across the skin. The white scratch burned, but no blood came up. Standing up and turning on the light, I looked for something more effective. I kicked an empty plastic bag and found a disposable razor. I smashed the flimsy plastic housing, exposing the blade. Holding my breath, I pressed the blade to my left wrist and pulled it across. Success! This cut was deep, painful, and red. A sense of relief bubbled up. I pulled the blade across the skin again. The blood made the blade and my fingers red. Again and again, I cut, trying to press it deeper into the flesh each time, but the skin was raw and ragged. I couldn't see where I was cutting.

Then I stopped and exhaled. I looked at the streetlight. The cuts stung, and although I was bleeding, it wasn't the gush of blood I had imagined. There were no tears on my cheeks, and no sound escaped my throat. Sadness wasn't the overwhelming feeling I was having. It was ugliness. As though there was an ugliness inside me that I wanted to bleed out. An ugliness fed by shame and unworthiness. I was ashamed of everything that I did and said. I wished I had stayed in my room tonight and every night so as not to embarrass myself. I hated feeling that way. Yet I also loved the world and people. I didn't know how to be in the world and not feel ashamed.

I picked up the blade and pressed it against the other wrist. With less force, I cut into my right wrist. The first cut was the most satisfying, the best. Each following cut accomplished less. Still, the pain in my wrists distracted me from the ugly feeling. Was that men's voices I heard outside on the street? No, that had been the night of the festival of San Juan. Tonight there was no one and nothing outside. I dropped the blade. My legs ached from crouching on the floor. As the blood began to dry on my wrists, the skin around the cuts tightened.

Why tonight of all nights had I done it? Tonight had not been any more heartbreaking than last night or last month. Why had I stopped? Was I one of those cutters? I understood the relief the cuts and blood brought, but I wasn't cutting to be cutting. I was tired of always failing.

I ripped a page out of my journal and wiped the blood off my wrists with the hard blank page. I dropped the bloody paper on the floor. Back on my mattress, I lay my head down on my pillow, and immediately after closing my eyes, I was asleep. I spent the night in a restless sleep full of dreams about dinosaurs chasing me across a field.

When I woke up, I flashed back to the question on the Peace Corps application. Have you ever been depressed or had thoughts of suicide? Hasn't everyone?! But I knew what the correct answer was, and that was the box I checked. No. While other mothers may have warned their children not to drink or take drugs, my mother warned me not to kill myself. We both knew that there were plenty of reasons to do it. The poverty and uncertainty of our lives kept me from seeing the future as a bright place full of possibilities. The empty boxes of wine stacked outside the garbage can were evidence that my mother had her own way of dealing with this life. One day my mother caught me watching a movie about teen suicide. As the perky redheaded suburban teen cried about her terrible life, my mother reminded me that my grandmother and she would be very upset if I killed myself. Both of my grandparents had cheered my successes and hugged me when I needed it. And as far as I was concerned, my grandmother was the reason the earth revolved around the sun. Sparing my family the shame and hurt kept me alive back in high school and college whenever different ideas slunk across my consciousness. Now my family was far away, and it cost fifty cents per minute on a static-filled line to speak to my mother or my grandmother.

I rose and cleaned up the razor and the broken plastic. On the street below, men walked to work, and cholitas in their voluminous skirts headed to the market to buy the day's groceries. I knew I was going to have to solve this problem for myself. Peace Corps was something I had wanted since high school. Maybe I was a failure in love and work, but I managed to get here and do what I dreamed of doing. I could not give up or give in. I took the blood-stained piece of paper off the floor, folded it up, and taped it to the inside of my journal. It would be a reminder of what I did. Otherwise, I would try to convince myself that it hadn't happened, that I was OK when I wasn't. I closed the book and put it on the floor.

I had to talk to someone. That was the promise I made myself. The official medical staff was out of the question because my service would be immediately terminated. I heard about volunteers being "psych vac'd" or evacuated back to DC for psychological reasons, and I imagined this would qualify. Peace Corps responded immediately whenever we had parasites in our intestines or injuries to our appendages, but I don't remember being told about options for counseling. Not that I would have spoken to anyone connected to the organization. I hated the thought of admitting what I did (and failed to do), but it was the only strategy I could think of to keep myself from doing it again. Laura was hundreds of miles away, and I didn't know when I would see her again. After everything I went through to get to Bolivia, I was determined to stay. Leaving would be failure.

I pulled on a thick sweater and walked down to the store for sugar and instant coffee. As I passed the post office, I noticed it was open. As wrecked as I was, I knew I had to go in and check for mail because it had been weeks since I had received anything.

"No, it hasn't arrived," the mailman said. He was wearing the same tan sweater he always wore. He frowned and asked, "Have you been crying?"

"No, I haven't," I said defiantly. I had been crying for hours, but I wasn't going to tell him that.

"Your eyes are red. You look terrible." He scrunched up his face. Then, having given his verdict, he turned and walked away. *How rude! Why, I should tell that man...*I stopped. I realized what a nice change it was to feel anger instead of despair for a moment.

I plodded through my days. Drinking my instant coffee, going to the Children's Center, and returning home in the afternoon. I chose long sleeves to hide the scabs on my skin. The scabs fell off, and the skin smoothed out. I went for hikes in the hills behind the Children's Center as often as I could get away. Walking had always been the best way to clear my head. All those weekend hikes in the Cascades with my mom taught me that there was no better way to stop obsessing about all the things wrong in my life than by ascending a hill on a dirt path.

A few weeks later, I found myself at Daniel's house after another Sunday afternoon of drinking chicha. I sat on the cement patio, and he worked in his tiny kitchen using only the fading sunlight. He chopped vegetables and sang to himself, not quietly but robustly as if he were an opera singer in front of a packed theater. His house was much smaller than mine but right off the square, near the center of everything. The patio was covered with buckets, too many chairs, and one single tree in the middle, but it was comfortable.

He was making grilled cheese sandwiches. The campo cheese was from the store run by nuns. Campo cheese was hard, salty, and dry, but when heated directly in the pan, it eventually softened and became stretchy. Crunchy and gooey at the same time. When I bit into the sandwich, the toasted bread scraped the top of my mouth, and a trickle of grease ran down my chin. It was slightly rubbery, but perfect for this chilly night. The sky revealed the southern constellation of stars, different from the constellations visible from North America, but still only stars twinkling in the sky. I watched Daniel eat his sandwich while he turned the pages of a magazine. I wondered whether he was the one I was supposed to tell. As soon as I thought it, I knew I had to do it. His life seemed to be a series of triumphs stretching out before him toward the horizon. Would he have any compassion for why I did it? There would be no better time than right now. I started to cry, sobbing through my mouth full of melted cheese.

"What's the matter? Is the cheese too hot?" he looked alarmed. I had never cried in front of him. I swallowed the mouthful of cheese and stopped crying. I was confessing my weakness, but I wanted to appear strong as I was doing it.

"OK, I'm going to tell you something, and you have to promise not to freak out," I said sternly. I couldn't believe I was about to tell this guy, the same charismatic, suave beauty whom I so distrusted when I arrived in Kantuta. The one who had warned me about getting too close before he even met me. But I could not stop.

"What's the matter?" he said calmly.

"I am not telling you this to make you feel sorry for me. I'm just doing this because I know I need to tell someone." He put down his sandwich on the stone table between us and looked at me.

"Two weeks ago, I tried to kill myself," I said, keeping my eyes focused on the cold cement floor in front of me. "Well, that makes it sound worse than it was. I slashed my wrists with a razor blade, but of course, I didn't do it right and was never in any real danger." I didn't want to give him a chance to say anything, so I kept talking, only occasionally peeking at his face to see whether he was watching me. He was. I told him I did not want anyone else to know what had happened because someone might think I needed to be sent home. He lit a cigarette, took a drag and then handed it to me. Rubbing the back of his neck distractedly, he blew smoke up into the air above him. I talked about what I should have done, filling up the space with as many words as possible. I was trying to show that I was in control and not to cry, but that's when I started crying again, harder. Daniel walked over to my seat and hugged me. The shame made me want to get up and walk away. I was relieved when he walked back to his seat.

"I'm...ah...I'm not sure what to say. Are you OK now?" I nodded my head yes. I exhaled and calmed down a little. He looked me in the eyes and asked what I wanted him to do. He had already done it by listening to me, by letting me talk. He promised not to tell anyone.

"But you have to promise me you won't do that again." I nodded. He asked to see the cuts on my wrist. I shook my head and pulled my sleeves down. I did not want him to look at them because maybe they wouldn't be as ugly as he expected. Maybe he wouldn't believe me. Or maybe he would and decide I needed professional help.

A slow Chet Baker song played on the tiny black Brazilian stereo. I had given him that tape. The smell of stale tobacco stung my nose, but the sensation of pressing my lips together, inhaling, and blowing out kept me from thinking about how much I had revealed. I hadn't considered how he would react, only that I had to tell him. I didn't want him to try to fix it. Telling him was part of how I was fixing it. I never wanted to burden anyone with the true details of my life.

Our cigarette smoke drifted upward. The tree in the center of his patio swayed in the wind, and I felt a chill. Except for the rustling tree leaves, the town was quiet. I carried our dishes into the kitchen. Suddenly, I was exhausted.

"Do you want me to walk you home?" he said as I put my coat on.

"No, it's still early. I think I'll be OK." I squeezed his shoulder and walked out into the plaza.

13

La Aislamiento — Isolation

At 2 a.m., I awoke to the sound of knocking on my door. Then someone yelled my name from the street. I jumped out of my mosquito net, pissed off because I assumed it was some drunk playing tricks on the gringa. Whom did I see but my friend Laura standing next to her enormous floral-print suitcase on the cobblestone street below my window.

"Oh my god! Wait, I'll be right down," I yelled. I hadn't seen her in months and couldn't believe she was in Kantuta. When we hugged, she still smelled like an expensive fragrance despite having been on a bus for hours.

"What are you doing here?" I helped her bring everything up to my room.

"I've been sick for the last few weeks, so they sent me to La Paz to make sure I didn't have typhoid fever. Yesterday, they told me it was OK to go home. I decided to take a detour to see you."

We talked nonstop until 4 a.m. She updated me on her project, what she thought of the new crop of volunteers that had arrived, and all the gossip about who was sleeping with whom.

I went to work for a few hours while she slept. I thought about telling Laura about cutting my wrists. Right after it happened, I wrote her a letter that I never sent. But I didn't want to have to tell anyone that story again, not even her. I hoped to keep it a secret for the rest of my life.

Over dinner, I asked her what she wanted to do after Peace Corps.

"Maybe urban planning. I'm not sure I want to be an interior designer anymore. I never thought I'd enjoy working on this big sewer project as much as I did. It was fun to tell construction workers what to do. What about you?"

"Sometimes I think I'd like to get into publishing—you know, like be an editor or writer. But I don't know how a person does that or even what kind of degree I'd need."

"I could totally see you doing that," she said. "You already LOOK like an editor, with those glasses and everything." I pushed my heavy government-issue black-rimmed glasses up the bridge of my nose in an attempt to look as scholarly as possible, and we laughed.

Laura left the next day, but not before we made plans to travel to Brazil after our service ended. We promised to help each other lose fifteen pounds before the end of service so that we could wear bikinis on the beach in Brazil. I went back to my quiet room tired but feeling heartened by her visit.

Three weeks later, a boy from the telephone office told me I had a call from Laura.

"They kicked me out," she sobbed. "Someone found out I took an extra week returning to my site and they considered it an illegal vacation. I didn't lie when they asked me. Now I have to go home." My lungs suddenly deflated. I couldn't believe it—not that she took a few days of illegal vacation but that she was being terminated for it. Volunteers took illegal vacation all the time. The star volunteers, the ones the administration loved to talk about, were some of the worst offenders and would disappear for weeks. They knew how to work the system and never get caught. But my best friend, the only Latina in the group, was being made an example of. It felt unfair.

"I will come to La Paz," I told her. I squeezed onto an express bus going through Kantuta that night, and two days later I was in La Paz, where I was relieved to find that Laura had calmed down. We spent a day in La Paz together, shopping for last-minute gifts, trying to pretend this was not a big deal. I couldn't believe she was leaving.

"I know I'll see you again, so don't even think about losing touch," I said as I hugged her good-bye in the morning before she took a cab to the airport. I wondered what I was going to do. The organization didn't seem to care about the implications of making an example of her. Maybe she was just unlucky. But brown people always seemed to get in trouble for the same behavior that white people were never punished for. I knew I had to stick it out. I would stay, but not for Peace Corps. Losing Laura would make this experience more difficult, but I wasn't going to give up.

Back in Kantuta, I decided to move into a bigger house. The room where I lived had too many bad memories. A few blocks away there was an apartment in a big house that had a kitchen and bathroom.

My new room was a little smaller, but much more private, and the inside patio was all mine. The only other person who ever used it was the saleslady who worked at the clothing store connected to the building. She was quiet, and smiled at me every morning.

In the evenings, I searched for radio stations, listening closely for a word of English. I wanted news from the outside world: an earthquake, a sex scandal, a cheesy story about a poor person who overcame adversity to become something special. Radio Kantuta was the town's only station. It came through loud and clear in Quechua. After a few minutes, I would realize how little Quechua I understood. Beyond the few words I knew, it made no sense to me. I loved the idea of learning it, even as I struggled with the grammar and pronunciation. Every new phrase was one more phrase that wasn't going to die. It was a reminder that Quechua was very much a living language, the language of a flourishing culture. I felt that way every time I learned a new Karuk word from my grandmother, who had learned those same words from her mother. But here in Kantuta, people spoke Spanish most of the time, and my Quechua became more of a performance piece, used to greet people and show them I was learning their language.

Daniel came to see my new place and showed up with cheap cigarettes and bottles of beer so we could christen the house. He had been working in the countryside for weeks. Neither one of us had been to Cochabamba for a long time, and, especially now that Laura was gone, it seemed as if he and I were the only two volunteers left in the country.

"What do you think would happen if you and I ever got together?" Daniel asked as he poured us both another glass of beer. It felt less like an attempted seduction and more as though he was presenting a business proposition. I thought about everything we had been through and the months remaining before he left.

"It would completely destroy our friendship." I looked at him.
A few months ago, I would have let his comment pass as though
I hadn't heard it, or I would have made a joke. But we were way
past that. "I would get self-conscious like I always do after casual
sex; you would disappear like you do and then show up one day
with a gorgeous woman; and we would pretend it never happened."
He didn't say anything. He knew this; I just had to say it out loud.
I finished my glass of beer. Had I ruined the relaxed mood of the
evening by being honest? Then I remembered that he was the one
who asked me. We finished our beers, and after an overly dramatic
yawn, he said he had to get home. I knew things would be fine
between us again eventually because we needed each other too
much not to get over it.

The next morning as I prepped for the day, I finally found the BBC
on my radio. I listened to the British voices tell me the news. Trouble in the Middle East, the rising cost of coffee, a plane crash with
no survivors—the world continued moving along, and it was comforting to hear English descriptions of it coming from the stereo.
This news felt immediate. I lingered a bit and fixed myself another
cup of instant coffee. That's when I heard something I hadn't heard
for almost a year: an American Indian speaking.

I froze. There it was, that distinctive way many American Indians in the West speak. The halting, slow speech pattern that I always
assumed I did not have until a white guy I dated in college kept
interrupting me. He said I took…too long…to finish…a…sen-
tence. He complained that he could never tell when I had finished

a thought and it was his turn to speak.

Had they mentioned what tribe she was from? The reporter said it was a tribe in Nevada; maybe she was Shoshone. In college I met some Shoshone ladies at a protest for Yucca Mountain. I was a student then, still figuring out whether it was more effective to fight the wrong I saw in the world or to contribute to the good. I thought I had to choose to do one or the other. Joining Peace Corps was a commitment to contribute to the good. With everything that had happened lately, I was no longer sure that was what I was doing.

"Since time immemorial," said the reporter. Oh no, did he really have to use that phrase? The reporter was interviewing the Native lady about an environmental issue, but it had been such a long time since I had heard an Indian speaking that I focused instead on the way she spoke. The reporter remarked about the broken-down cars and other signs of poverty surrounding the woman's house. The nasal tone was full of condemnation for a society that would let this happen, and pity for the Native woman. The story ended, and, thankfully, it wasn't followed up by depressing flute music. I put my hand on the on/off button, waiting, hoping there would be a follow-up story about another group of Natives. Hoping that the BBC was doing a whole day of programming about Natives. But no, next was a report on soccer. I sighed and turned off the radio. This unexpected reminder of the world back home was particularly bittersweet because there was no one here—not Daniel, not other Peace Corps volunteers, not Bolivians—who would understand what I was talking about when I mentioned hearing a Native American on the radio. I finished my coffee and headed out the door to the empty road for a jog. The Native woman's voice repeated in my head.

"Indian," I whispered, in that quick way my grandmother said it. The way the woman on the radio said it. IN-din. I repeated it over and over to prove to myself I knew how to say it like a Native. I said it low so that the older woman sweeping the sidewalk would not hear me as I passed by.

"Buen día," I heard her greet me. I nodded to acknowledge her and picked up my pace. I pushed myself to run instead of walk because I wanted to be alone on the path. Running through a dry creek bed, I passed the houses on the edge of town and followed the trail leading up the hill. Hearing the Native woman on the radio reminded me that I was missing more about the United States than hamburgers or bookstores full of books in English. I was missing powwows in smelly gyms and waiting in line for frybread. I even missed the way I felt when I saw glassy-eyed elders boarding a city bus, knowing they would continue to lead a hard life until their last days. There was a community back there in the US that I belonged to, and I missed it.

Reaching the crest of a hill, I stopped and hunched over, trying to catch my breath. I always forgot how hard it was to run at this altitude. Turning around, I saw Kantuta sitting in the valley. The two orange-ish church steeples marked the center of town, and red-tile roofs competed with corrugated-tin roofs and a few unfinished shells of buildings. I pressed my right hand to the stitch in my side. Kantuta was not a picturesque village like the one I saw in the guidebook I bought before coming to Bolivia. But it was full of streets I knew and buildings I entered every day. It meant something to me because I knew who and what was inside those buildings and on those streets. I had been given an opportunity to work with the children at the Center and live in this community, not by the US government, but by the Bolivians. While my friends back in the States were learning how to make a perfect café mocha or counting their pennies as they began graduate school, I was here doing this. Two years was a short time in the expanse that was my life. The outside world would always be there. My family and my community would also be there when I returned to the US. I turned around and headed back into the town.

14

La Celebración — The Celebration

It was the Festival of the Virgin of Candelaria, the patron saint of Kantuta. La Virgen de Candelaria was the darkest of patron saints. *La morenita*, she was called. Her image was first found on a rock by the Indigenous people of the Canary Islands off the coast of Spain. They immediately recognized her as one of their goddesses. When the Spanish colonizers came along, they decided she looked instead like a dark-skinned version of the Virgin Mary. A black Madonna. Like all successful colonizers, they knew the importance of putting their own stamp on the most important elements of a culture.

Throughout South America, this dark Virgin was revered; her smile was said to comfort the afflicted. In Kantuta, the Festival of the Virgin of Candelaria was the biggest festival of the year. Halloween plus Christmas topped with mounds of food and buckets of booze. Grown children returned home, families hosted huge parties that lasted for days, with endless alcohol and enough food for anyone who showed up. Every mass at the church was overflowing with people showing devotion to their saint, their town, their family. Maybe because Bolivians were normally reserved people, the exuberance they demonstrated during Candelaria seemed outsized and infectious.

One of the biggest events of the festival was the running of the bulls. It was not like the event in Spain, with locals and crazy tourists running through the streets chasing Hemingway's ghost. In Kantuta, bulls were rounded up and brought to a dirt pen the size of a football field. A fence of stacked crisscrossed wood surrounded the pen. It kept spectators out and the bulls in. Or at least it tried to keep them in. The bulls could easily charge through the wooden fences when they were moving fast. Inside the ring, men and boys ran from the sides and taunted the bulls. Sometimes they swung a red cape in a bull's face. Mostly they hurled their bodies straight toward an animal in hopes of getting a reaction. Around each bull's neck was a bag of money; the goal was to get close enough to snatch it away. Chicha, testosterone, and heart-thumping fear propelled each of the competitors across the dusty field into a bull's path. The bulls often gored or trampled them. Sometimes a man even managed to grab the money, and the crowd cheered.

When Daniel came to tell me we were invited to a party hosted by one of Kantuta's families, I wasn't sure if I wanted to go. Despite (or maybe because of) the cheers and laughter erupting out of every home in Kantuta, I wanted to hide in my mosquito net.

"Come on—it's my LAST Candelaria," Daniel said. He knew me. He knew that my natural instinct was to hide away in my room. And he knew exactly what would make me feel obliged to join him at the party. Daniel had helped me through my darkest moments in Kantuta, and if he needed a plus-one for this party, I was going. The thick flannel shirt I wore made me look like a lumpy Eddie Vedder. I didn't care.

The party had started hours, maybe days, earlier. What looked like a hundred people milled around a large open patio. Everywhere there was high-pitched laughter, stacks of empty glasses, half-full bottles of whisky, and general chaos. This patio was the heart of the home. I had one like it in my rented house, but it never felt alive and warm. In the center of this patio was a charming little arbor with grapevines winding up the sides. In the corner under a single bare bulb sat a drummer, an accordion player, and a guitar player. I sunk into a seat and decided to give this party a chance.

The hosts handed Daniel and me small glasses of chicha. After splashing the customary drop of milky yellow liquid onto the cement to share with Pachamama, I lifted the full glass to my lips. The strong fermented smell made my mouth water. I took a breath, then gulped it down. Sour then sweet, this was quality stuff, made especially for Candelaria. This was followed by champagne, then whisky, and something else which might have been a rum and Coke. I wasn't sure.

"Seco," the man ordered as he handed me each drink. He was asking me to drain the glass and leave it dry. I was at the mercy of the host's militant generosity. As gringos in Kantuta, we were considered important guests, and it was a priority to share what they had with us.

I heard drums beating and cymbals crashing from the street. The sound got louder and louder until I realized an actual marching band was coming in through the front door, pushing us up against one another and making a deafening joyous noise. I loved marching bands and stood there vibrating with the music coming from the horns and the boom of the drum. They circled the patio and then filed out the door in a straight line. I touched Daniel's shoulder and smiled my biggest goofiest smile. He nodded back. This was a party.

"Ursula, we're going to dance later," I heard a voice say before I knew who was speaking. It was a guy sitting half in the shade and half in sunlight on the other side of the patio. It was difficult to see his features clearly. Only his dark wispy goatee, almond eyes, and black hair stood out. His name escaped me, but there was something familiar about his face. I forced a polite smile. I did not feel like dancing. As fun as the party might be, I planned on leaving once I met my duty as a friend.

The accordion player stuck his arms into the instrument's straps, and the band began to play. One of the older men walked up to me and held out his upturned hand. I did not want to dance. It had been a rough couple of months, and things were starting to get better, but I still felt vulnerable. If there was one affliction I wanted to light a candle for at the Virgin's mass, it would be my loneliness. And I knew that once Daniel left, invitations to parties like this might not come anymore.

The white-haired man kept motioning me toward the dance floor, encouraging me to join him. The music was loud, and the booze was warming my insides. It was a party and my last Candelaria as well. I was a guest, and sitting on the side with a frown would have been rude. And why the hell did I join Peace Corps if I wasn't going to take part? I stood up, took his hand, and walked into the center of the patio where everyone was dancing. He laughed, swung me around, and attempted to lead. I was never very good at following.

A seat opened up on the other side of the patio, and I saw the guy who'd promised we would dance, leaning in to talk to the woman sitting next to him. She had short, dark hair and was no traditional cholita, wearing the thin polyester skirt and blouse of a modern Bolivian woman. There was something familiar about her, and she seemed to recognize me, but I could not figure out where I knew her from. I nodded in her direction, and she replied with a slight smile.

"Your husband?" I asked, motioning to him.

"We are not married," he said before she could answer. Two small children ran up and huddled around talking to her. The band began to play again, and I could not hear anything else that he said. Her lips curled into a rumpled smirk. We seemed to be sharing a laugh as if he were her flirty boyfriend and his behavior was annoying yet expected. I had seen this before. Flirtatious husbands sitting next to their wives, but it always seemed to be a joke. Their wives would chastise them with a quick swat, and we would all laugh. There was even a popular song about a husband who tries to cheat on his wife but keeps getting denied, and in the end returns to his wife. Daniel laughed as he crossed the dance floor with a pretty young woman. In a few months, Kantuta would be part of his past. I had nine months left in Kantuta, but knew it was going to be less interesting without him.

The air cooled down as afternoon became evening. I was glad my layers of flannel protected me. Strings of small twinkling lights hanging across the patio suddenly flicked on and made the dance floor magical and bright. I was about to slurp down another cup of chicha when I saw the Bolivian man toasting me with his own cup. He was persistent; I had to give him that. I toasted him back and drank it down, barely tasting the bitterness as I handed the glass back and wiped the last drops off my lips with my finger.

Then dinner arrived. Like all good Bolivian hosts, they made massive amounts of food: rice and a spicy sauce, potatoes, and chicken. Thank God for the meal, because with each glass of chi-cha, I was getting wobblier. I needed food. I joined Daniel eating his plate of rice and chicken at the back of the patio. We sat there in silence, savoring our food and enjoying the moment.

A cueca came on, and I grabbed Daniel. Cueca was the tradi-tional Bolivian folk dance, and everyone crowded onto the patio. The memory of the plump white anthropologist bobbing around during training teaching us the cueca flashed in my head. In train-ing, this had seemed like a quaint custom, something nervous chil-dren demonstrated on a stage for "Indigenous day." But this dance was alive. We circled each other on the crowded patio, laughing and making exaggerated moves. Everyone else twirled napkins, but we shook our hands as we danced.

The guy with the goatee finally asked me to dance. I looked for approval from the woman who'd been with him, but she was dancing with someone else. I decided to follow him. It was hard to guess anyone's age in Bolivia because even young people looked weathered, but I guessed he was about twenty-eight like me. He began by leading, taking a step and expecting me to follow. I was surprised when he responded with flexibility as I took a step in my own direction instead of following his lead.

"You know how to dance well," he said, not leaning in too closely, as we sat down. I rolled my eyes and smirked. I was a ter-rible dancer and knew it. We chatted while not getting too close. Fernando was his name. Someone brought us glasses of beer, and as we sat he told me that his brother had attended the Children's Center when he was younger and how it had helped him when times were tough. I had only been half listening to him, but this caught my attention.

"Your brother? Was at the same Center where I work?" I asked.

He nodded his head yes. No one had ever admitted this to me. In Kantuta, the Children's Center was seen as a place for poor kids from the countryside. There were plenty of townspeople who received help, but not once did anyone tell me that the Center had helped someone in his or her family. Was that where I'd seen Fernando before?

"El es tu dueño?" he leaned in close, and I felt his face brush against my hair. He pulled back and motioned with his chin toward Daniel. He was asking whether Daniel was my *dueño*, which literally means "owner." This was a common word for boyfriend that I had heard many times. I recognized the casual sexism in the term, but at that moment, with the alcohol lighting me up from inside and his dark eyes staring into mine, I wasn't about to launch into some takedown of the hidden gender bias in his word choice.

"Amigos, no más," I said as we watched Daniel dancing.

The band played the first few lines of a cueca, and Fernando pointed to the dance floor. I hesitated, not sure what to do. Even if he had a girlfriend, wife, or whatever, this was innocent. Hot, but innocent. I told myself I was just storing images and generating fantasies I could recall later when I was alone in my mosquito net. I might as well enjoy the moment, take this opportunity. I looked around for Daniel, but he was already with someone else.

Fernando led me to the center of the crowd, already starting the cueca. As the song swelled, he patted down his pockets in search of the requisite napkin. The cueca required accessories—specifically, a napkin to twirl in the air. My pockets were empty too, and by now all the people around us had found a napkin. He stopped moving, touched my hand, and pointed upwards. I looked up and realized we were dancing under the grape arbor. With everyone swirling around us, he reached up over my head and gently plucked two small leaves. The sweet smell of the grape broke over us. He stepped in closer and handed me the tender green leaf. We stood together like that for a moment. The hairs on the back of my neck stood up as I took the delicate little leaf from his hand. I thought of myself as immune to romance, a hardened woman who was realistic about everyone's true motives. But this worked. It was romantic and cheesy, but also sweet. He winked, and I tried to hide my smile by looking down. We twirled our leaves around in the air. The woman he was with was gone by the time we sat down. I remained on the floor with him for every dance.

With each passing moment, I was more interested. I stopped looking away coyly as he stared at me. Things had never gone well with a Bolivian man for this long. It had been a very long time since things had gone this well with a man from any continent, for that matter. This was fun. Unadulterated joy.

"Me aceptas o no?" he asked, his arm resting on the back of my chair as we took a break. His voice was scratchy. He was asking me if I accepted him, but I didn't exactly understand what he meant. I looked into his lovely face and thought of a number of things I would be willing to accept from him right at that moment. None of which he could give me here on this crowded patio. I sighed.

I held up my index finger to tell him I would be right back. Daniel was standing by the door sharing a cigarette with an old man.

"Daniel, do you think it would be safe to take one of these guys home with me tonight?" I leaned against the door and asked him. I phrased it as a question because it seemed too bold to simply tell him that I was taking someone back to my house. The truth was, I had never taken a stranger home with me before. Never ever. Not in Bolivia or in the United States. The Movie Channel's repeated showings of *Looking for Mr. Goodbar* right about the time I reached puberty had traumatized me. Imagine being a thirteen-year-old girl watching Diane Keaton getting killed by a stranger she had picked up at a bar. I limited my casual dalliances to men I knew.

"Which one?" Daniel asked, his eyes only opening halfway. I motioned with my head back at Fernando. Daniel tried to focus his eyes in the general direction.

"Darling, I think you should take several of these guys home with you," he said. Daniel turned to the old man and asked in Spanish, "Right!?" They both threw their heads back and laughed.

"Are you OK?" I asked. He motioned with his cigarette toward the door, but did not answer. He lived one block away, and I wondered whether I should help him get home. Part of me wanted to tell him to come by in an hour to make sure I was still alive. But I knew he'd be passed out by then.

I walked back to my seat next to Fernando. I motioned with my head toward the door. The wide-eyed look he gave me might have been shock. Maybe Bolivian women didn't do this. At least not Bolivian women in Kantuta where everyone lives at home until they get married. I was not a Bolivian woman. It would not be a good idea for either of us to be seen leaving the party together, so we left separately.

We stumbled to my house. I shut the door quietly behind us in case my neighbors were home. The dancing and food had sobered me up a little, and I felt I needed to keep my wits about me. There were all those warnings to watch out for lecherous men who seduced gringas, and here I was dragging a Bolivian man into my empty house. Did that make *me* the letch?

I fumbled for the keys to my room as his eyes darted nervously from my hand on the door to my face. He was as anxious about this as I was. Was this how the men at the running of the bulls felt before they walked out into the ring? He stepped close enough for me to feel his breath on my neck. Any guilt I felt about what I was doing faded as he put his arms around my waist and kissed me. The pins in the lock released, and we pushed through the door. My room was dark except for the light from the streetlight coming through the window. I could feel him more than I could see him.

We sat on the hay mattress that doubled as my couch. We went at it, greedily grasping handfuls of flesh, kissing and unbuttoning in an uncoordinated rush to get to the good stuff. I reached under his shirt and ran my hands up his bare stomach and chest. He was smooth and strong. He pulled his shirt over his head and threw it down. He tried to kiss me deeply, and I resisted, turning my head. Here I was with this gorgeous man in my room, all to myself. What was I waiting for? But I wanted to take a microsecond. I had to make sure I wanted this. I was sober enough to realize that this was no small thing. There were implications beyond this room. It took me half a second to decide that oh my God of course I wanted this. I turned my face and pressed my lips against his. I took off the layers of flannel and khaki clothes that had been protecting me all night. As he started to untie his boots, I stuck my hand out and stopped him.

"You have to leave your boots on," I told him. I had instantly decided it would be less serious if he kept his boots on. He complied, and, now that he was unhindered by any clothing except his unlaced boots, I pulled him toward me. A stalk of hay from the mattress stuck me in the butt but was immediately forgotten. This was not about foreplay or slowly getting to know each other's bodies. This was about getting as close as possible to another human being while keeping a few steps ahead of my conscience.

The smell of his strong, sweet cologne mixed with the scent of the cheap cigarettes we had shared all night. It reminded me of boys at junior high school dances. They doused themselves in cologne, then awkwardly pressed in to me as Loverboy and Foreigner blasted from tinny speakers. I had been careful with those boys, never going further than a few kisses and gropes. I knew everyone expected me to follow my mother's example and become a pregnant teenager, but I had no intention of fulfilling their preconceived notion. I clutched Fernando's torso tightly, closed my eyes, and stopped worrying about what this all meant. His strong legs pressed against mine. He kissed me deeply, and I pressed every part of my body into his. I tried to hold it there for as long as possible.

"Oh my God, I needed that," I said in English afterwards. He laughed. I smiled even though I had no idea whether he understood me. I wasn't joking. Over the last few months, I had started to feel like an alien. Lonely but surrounded by people. I would probably never see him again, but I was here with him now, and I was grateful. At this moment, my identity didn't matter—who I was, who I wanted to be. The weight of trying to change something, help someone, was lifted, and I was simply another human being. We lay next to each other on the lumpy mattress as he ran his finger down the length of my arm. He kissed me and stood up. He dressed and tucked in his shirt.

"Are you an athlete?" I asked, in Spanish.

"I play soccer," he said and mimed kicking the ball into the goal.

"I sometimes jog, out at the landing strip." I had no idea why

I said that. I was nervous and, never having been in this situation before, unsure of what to say. I dressed quickly and stood up, hoping he would understand that it was time to leave.

"I know; I've seen you," he said, and kissed me. He'd seen me? Then I remembered who I was in this town. Of course he knew who I was. I may have felt unimportant and invisible, but because I was from the United States, I most definitely was visible. I walked him to my front door and peeked out to see whether anyone was there. The yellow light illuminated an empty street. With a quick nod, he stepped through the doorway. I looked the other direction to make sure no one saw him. By the time I looked back, he'd disappeared around the corner. It was the middle of the night, but as his steps grew fainter, I heard the sound of a band playing a few blocks away.

The next morning, I made my instant coffee as strong as instant coffee gets. Two scoops. Standing on my patio, listening to the nearby shopkeeper pull open the gate to his store, I suddenly remembered how I knew Fernando. I had met his wife, the woman who had been sitting next to him earlier in the night. She had worked at the store located in the same building as my old apartment. One day I came home from work after a rainstorm to discover all of my laundry missing from the clothesline where I had left it. She emerged from the back of the store holding one of my shirts. She had brought in the laundry I had hung on the line that morning. She had saved my clothes from the rain. I thanked her, but felt a little embarrassed at the thought of her folding my panties and bras. We never spoke. I vaguely remembered a dark-haired man passing through the patio some mornings as I drank down the first of my three daily cups of coffee. I was probably dressed in shorts that barely covered my ass and braless under a half-buttoned shirt. An outfit no Bolivian woman would have worn if any man could see her. And now I had screwed that nice woman's husband. I closed my eyes and shook my head. What had I done?

Last night it had all seemed random. A hot guy at a party on a night when I was feeling lonely. But maybe he knew who I was. Then I remembered what his first word had been to me. "Ursula." He had said my name. He knew exactly who I was. And I had only seen him as another Bolivian guy.

A few days later, the final running of the bulls was held at the large pen on the north edge of town. Daniel had entered the ring and managed to pull the necklace full of cash that was attached to the bull's neck. He'd always wanted to do it, and although the money was less than the cost of one bottle of booze, his chest puffed up with pride.

Of course, I told him everything about my night with Fernando. I had to tell someone, and he was the only one in town who could safely keep my secret. He laughed, but before long was making lewd jokes. I dropped the subject. Had I done something wrong? This surprised me. Among the male volunteers, getting together with Bolivian women was a competition. How many parties had I attended where a gorgeous Bolivian woman arrived on the arm of some short, pale volunteer with stringy hair? Daniel often appeared with Bolivian women so stunning that they looked as though they'd walked off the stage of the Ms. Universe pageant. For the female volunteers, it was different. A female volunteer involved with a Bolivian man was assumed to be weak and insecure or else just passing time. But our dating options were limited. In small towns like Kantuta, most Bolivian men over eighteen were married. Gossip from other volunteers told me I was not the first woman to spend the night with a married Bolivian.

Still, I struggled with what I had done. I thought of myself as a principled person. A nice person. At least I had been. I occupied a unique position of power in this little Bolivian town that I never had back in the United States. In the US I was always the poorest, least-connected person of anyone I knew. I filed the paperwork for the important people or cared for their children while they did meaningful work. Here, by contrast, I had more education, resources, and money than most people, especially most women. This power was like an ill-fitting suit I wore for a job I was not sure how to do. I hoped that I wasn't using my privileged place in this community to break a rule I found inconvenient.

After several days, the Candelaria celebrations ended, and I went back to work. On my way home that first day, I heard someone say my name. A man. I turned and did not see anyone. I backtracked and looked around the corner. Standing inside the little store where I often bought cookies was a young man whom I recognized from the Center. He greeted me again and asked if I needed anything from the shelves. I shook my head and walked away. I thought it had been Fernando. I realized I was looking for him around every corner. In the mornings, I spent a little more time brushing my hair and was careful to wear clothing that was clean. I wanted to see him again.

In the days that followed, I had plenty of time to contemplate what my interest in Fernando might mean. Time to weigh the pros and cons of beginning a relationship with a married man less than a year before the end of my service. But I didn't spend my time contemplating. I spent it thinking about how much I wanted to get him back to my dusty little room, take off his clothes, and press into him. I found myself flirting with inanimate objects. Tomatoes and trees. I wanted to be prepared when I saw him. *My, how firm and red you are,* I thought as I looked at a ripe tomato. The eucalyptus trees lining the airport runway where I jogged received my best pouty side glance. Teresa asked me why I was smiling. I shrugged my shoulders and mumbled something about the weather. Ximenita assumed it had something to do with Daniel. I let her believe that, because I'd rather have her think that than know the truth. I had never acted this goofy. Something had bubbled up in me, and I wanted to enjoy the feeling, not think about its significance.

On a Friday morning, I walked through the front gate of the Children's Center at my customary 9:30 a.m. arrival time. A planned trip to Cochabamba that evening to see friends was distracting me. I wasn't thinking about Fernando. I nearly tripped on a rock when I saw him walking toward me. He was leaving the director's office. Thank goodness I had practiced my flirting, because I was able to flash him a smoldering look almost immediately. He returned my look with a deep stare that gave me goose bumps. Obviously, he had been practicing on something besides tomatoes and trees.

Seeing him for the first time in the daylight, I looked at his face without the haze of alcohol or the shadows of a poorly lit patio. He was gorgeous: dark eyes that I couldn't turn away from, raven-black hair, and smooth brown skin a few shades darker than my own. *Brown as a berry*, as my grandmother used to call me in the summer. We shook hands, and he stepped in close to kiss the air next to my cheeks in a proper Bolivian greeting. His hands were warm and rough.

"How are you today, señorita?" he asked with a formality that amplified the excitement of the moment.

"Fine, and yourself?" I said, trying not to smile too broadly. My heart was pounding. I didn't know what to do with my hands now that he wasn't touching them.

"I came to talk to the director about my brother," he motioned to the closed door behind him.

"Did you have a good Candelaria?" I asked. He laughed. I was proud that I had managed to do more than mumble and sweat.

"Best celebration in years." I bit my lower lip and exhaled. He said, "I came by your house the other day, but no one was home." I did a quick check to make sure no one was standing near us.

"I'm going to Cochabamba tonight. I will be home until 9 p.m." I was trying to drop the hint that I wanted him to come over. He did not react to my invitation, and I wondered whether I was using the wrong word or the wrong verb tense. Unaccustomed to playing hard to get in any language, I decided to be more direct with my invitation.

"Ven a mi casa," I said. Come to my house. What was I doing? He smirked and told me he would stop by later. We said good-bye, and he shook my hand gently and kissed my cheek for a few extra seconds, then stepped toward the street. I watched him leave through the gate. My thought was more *Oh boy* than *Oh no, what have I done?* The rest of the day, I hummed with anticipation while also trying to keep from getting my hopes up. I wanted so badly to confide in Ximenita, because I knew she would relish every detail of the interaction. But I would have to keep my mouth shut.

My bags were packed and ready before dinner. As the sky was turning from light to dark blue, the way it gets in the first hours of the evening, I heard a knock. I peeked between the door slats and saw Fernando looking left at something in the street, combing his hair down with his fingers. My stomach tightened with anticipation, and I did a mini-jig of happiness before undoing the metal latch and pulling the wood door open wide enough to let him in. It creaked as I shut it. I slid the latch back into the locked position as quietly as I could. The building was empty and silent except for us. The neighbors who also rented rooms in this building were not home, but they might arrive at any moment. I exhaled to calm myself. I was nervous, sure, but it was less about being with a married man than simply about being with *someone*. I had already started to forget that he was married. Maybe *forget* is not the right word. Maybe *ignore* is better. I had no animosity toward his wife; I had nothing except a desire to not know about her.

Inside the room, I reached up and pulled closed the drapes. They weren't real drapes, only more of the brightly colored cloth that I used for everything from tablecloths to laundry bags. The dim light from outside my window made his face darker and his hair like night.

"Hola," I said, crossing my arms awkwardly over my breasts in the least sexy pose I could have taken. He looked directly into my eyes and gently cupped the side of my face with his hand. I leaned into it, pressing my cheek into his open palm. It was rough, warm, and slightly damp. No one had touched my face for what seemed years. My tits, my ass, the spot in the middle of my back underneath where my bra hooks—sure, those places had been touched a few times. But there had not been this caress of my face. His other hand untucked my shirt, and he reached under the fabric to grasp my bare flesh.

"I have been thinking about you," he whispered. We were close now, and I smelled that same sweet cologne I remembered from our first night together. It was cheap cologne, and although it was too strong for my taste, it was his smell. I undid the top button of his shirt, then the next, until his smooth chest was open and exposed.

"I…thought about you too." I fumbled around in my mind for a better follow-up, but standing there, nervous and aroused, I could think of nothing. Then I remembered: this was an affair. The rules were different. I did not have to sound smart or hip, or prove anything. We were both here to have sex, as much sex as possible. Coyness was not necessary. What a relief! He kissed me with open hard lips, filling my mouth with his tongue. Then I pulled him into the open mosquito net encasing my bed, onto my unmade mattress. I did not have a bed frame or box springs, only a mattress inside a mosquito net and a thin sheet. That was all I needed.

"Urr," he whispered in my ear, softly pressing his tongue against the top of his mouth to roll out that r. No one had ever said my name that way. It sounded natural, yet different and new. I wanted him to say it again, but I also wanted him to stop talking so he could kiss me. This was the opposite of loneliness. This was the connection I had wanted.

15
Aventura — Adventure

Walking into the Children's Center for the first time in two weeks after taking some time off and traveling for required medical checkups, I was greeted by hugs from the little kids and handshakes from the older teenagers. I hadn't thought I would miss them as much as I had. When Tomas and Umberto came through the gate, I hugged Tomas. Umberto let me shake his hand. Then they ran off toward the kitchen where breakfast was being served.

I went into the kitchen, where Ximenita was ladling hot *maizena* into cups. It was my least favorite breakfast because it tasted like cornstarch and water, but I had learned to drink it, especially on cold mornings.

"Did you hear that Nilda is thinking about not wearing a cholita skirt anymore?" Ximenita asked. Nilda had recently moved from the campo and started working at the Center. She couldn't have been more than seventeen years old. It had been over a year since Ximenita had stopped wearing a pollera, and I wondered what she thought of Nilda's decision.

"That's sad, but I understand why." I looked at Ximenita, who turned to fill a tray of waiting cups. I didn't know Nilda well and wondered why Ximenita had told me this information. Maybe she wanted me to understand that she wasn't the only one who had made that choice. Nilda's situation was a reminder that even though there were elements of Indigenous Bolivian culture that were thriving, the pressure to conform in order to be successful still existed, and women like Nilda and Ximenita had to deal with it every day.

In the corner, I noticed a huge white freezer. The newness and brilliancy stood out amid the stained buckets and cans surrounding it.

"We brought it all the way from Cochabamba," Simon, the Center director, said, puffing up a little. It was a donation, or paid for by a donation, from the German evangelical organization that supported the Center. Often the kids asked me to translate the neat German handwriting on the back of postcards featuring pictures of giant cathedrals or perfectly coiffed frauleins. I had forgotten most of what I had learned in high school German class except numbers and a list of prepositions. I translated the few words I recognized, and guessed at the others. Together we arrived at a message that sounded like what a First World evangelical donor would want to deliver to its Third World charity recipient.

No matter the real message—I imagined the postcards said, *Don't give up hope; there's a rich white person on the other side of the planet praying for you.* Were there late-night television commercials in Germany with pictures of Tomas or Joaquin looking sad and dirty, with a voiceover asking for donations to help them? When I saw the Center children laughing, looking happy and full, I wondered whether the donors wanted to see pictures of that. I did not know the word for *charity* in German.

Simon rubbed his hand across the smooth white surface. I peeked inside the freezer and saw that it was barely cold and completely empty.

"We should use this to sell popsicles," Joaquin suggested. He was one of the older kids at the Center and a year away from graduating. Nora and Jennifer, two teenage girls who had helped with the bakery project, jumped up and down in excitement. Everybody with a refrigerator in town used it to make something to sell.

"I will pay for the sugar and mix if you'll let us use this freezer." Again committing my own resources was not something I should be doing, but I knew he didn't have extra cash to spend on such a project. His eyes narrowed.

"Señorita, this freezer is going to be full of the best quality of meat, fruits, milk, and maybe even cheese. I do not think there will be any room for your products," he said, his hand in the air making a dismissive gesture. A year and a half ago I would have turned and walked away, feeling dejected. A year and a half ago I wouldn't have even thought this idea was big enough for me to spend time on. But I had learned that starting a project at the Center required several steps. Simon would dismiss the idea at first. But I'd keep asking him, making jokes about the size of meat he planned on buying, or showing him how small a space we needed. Doña Florencia, his wife and the Center's cook, was my friend. She was the one who could help me get his approval. A week later, he called me into his office and told me we could use a small corner of the freezer for the popsicles.

Nora and Jennifer, the teenage girls who had been enthusiastic about the idea, led me to the market down the street. It was

Wednesday, not a busy day at the market, but the girls knew right where to find the tiny plastic bags, the sugar, and the flavor mix. Ximenita, the cook's assistant, helped us boil the water to make a few test popsicles.

"They worked, they worked!" Nora told me when I walked in the next morning. Simon was already halfway through one of first popsicles by the time I made it to the freezer. The following Saturday after breakfast, a few of the girls who had helped me with the bakery and two boys whom I didn't know well joined me in the Children's Center kitchen. We made four dozen popsicles and stuffed them into the tiny real estate we had been granted in the freezer. Standing in the kitchen with the kids, I looked up to see Ximenita smile and wink at me. She had been with me since my first day at the Center a year and a half earlier and knew how much I had struggled in those first few months.

On Sunday, market day, the cook let me in right after breakfast. Two of the younger kids had volunteered to sell the popsicles. They were probably about twelve years old, but had experience selling their mothers' baked goods. Nora and I handed the kids a tray full of popsicles and some coins to make change. I watched them disappear into the crowd surrounding the stalls of bread and backpacks and anything a person would want to buy. Within two hours, they sold everything we had. I carefully locked the money away in the cash box and said good-bye to Ximenita as I headed home. In the weeks to come, the kids would make twice as many popsicles in each batch and sell all of them.

What surprised me was what they did with the money. They bought enough oranges for the whole Center and passed them out to the kids one afternoon. They also bought an iron for their clothes. My Bolivian friends always looked put together, and no one left the house with wrinkly clothes. The kids from the Center often wore used clothes made thin by years of hand washing, but most of them were careful to keep their clothes as wrinkle-free as possible. Joaquin, who was tall and thin, waved his arm with a grand flourish and made sure I noticed the crease in his pants. I thought of all the times I had arrived in a rumpled dress pulled from the floor. What did they think of me when they watched me leave my apartment looking as though I had slept in my clothes? It was one of the things that made it clear that no matter how many commonalities existed due to our shared heritage, we were different. This had been the case all along, but only now was I starting to see myself through their eyes.

A few weeks later, Daniel asked me whether I knew the anthropologist who lived a few towns over. There were so many anthropologists in Bolivia that it was difficult to keep them straight sometimes.

"The one who loves goats?" Daniel asked as he stuffed shirts and jeans into his stained backpack. Now I remembered. She was having a *despedida* that weekend. "I can't go, but you should," he said. Despedidas were going-away parties that often turned into final blowout celebrations. After my recent trips, I was enjoying lying low in Kantuta. A party in another town sounded like too much effort.

I walked with Daniel to the corner where he was about to catch the late-night bus to La Paz for his Close of Service conference. Three days of meetings and workshops to prepare for the end of volunteers' service, to think about what they might do after they returned home. The end of my service was six months away. Or a hundred years. It was too far away to be real.

"Unless you're doing something with what's-his-name." Daniel looked at me. He did not approve of my relationship with Fernando. At first, he had encouraged me to go for it. But when he found out that Fernando was married, his opinion changed.

"We don't make plans. It's not like that," I said, shifting in the chair, trying to find a comfortable position. Daniel did not understand what Fernando gave me. I knew I wasn't going to change his mind that night or probably any night before he left Bolivia.

"Come on—this is supposed to be an adventure. Do something adventurous!" He cocked his head and smiled. I narrowed my eyes at him. He was presenting a challenge. Now I had to prove I was adventurous too. Jack Kerouac to his Dean Moriarty. My idea of adventure was tamer than his and usually included multiple backup plans.

I retreated to the dark behind my closed door and listened to the hum of the bus as it drove away. Maybe I should go to the party. Other volunteers would be there, friends whom I hadn't seen for weeks. It might be fun to be anonymous for a few hours again. Everyone in Kantuta knew me. When I first arrived, that made me feel special, like a celebrity. Now, it was exhausting. All the extra effort it took to be conscious of my actions, who might be watching me, and how they would judge me. In the United States, I was invisible most of the time. No one asked for my opinion, and even in small classes my college professors never knew who I was. I only spoke when I thought there was something important to be said. Twenty-seven years spent being invisible and silent, and now I was watched every second outside my house.

I decided to go to the party. While getting ready that morning, I listened to the radio. Radio Kantuta had recently given Fernando a morning spot. It was the first time I thought about how he made his living. He read the news in Quechua. I understood every few words, enough to make out that it was an announcement of a community meeting. I stood in the middle of the patio, sipping my coffee, glad that no one was there to see me suspended, marveling at my connection to the station that had felt like a barrier to me for the last year.

By nine, I was standing in the open-air market on the north side of town waiting for a ride. Dark clouds full of rain were moving in my direction. *Adventure*, I reminded myself. The flat cement floor of the market was empty except for the few women who sold onions and tomatoes every day of the week. A short man in a misshapen felt hat pulled large wood crates down from the back of his truck. My favorite food seller flipped her puffed pastries in hot oil. She was my favorite because she remembered my name and that I liked the sweet pastries the best. Sometimes being noticed had its advantages. I liked to get one of them right as it came out of the oil, when it was almost too hot to touch, and rip it apart piece by piece until there was nothing left but my sticky fingers.

I was tempted to walk over and buy something warm and greasy. Then I heard the rain. Softly at first as it hit the branches of the trees, then loudly as it pelted the roof of the market and poured off the corners of the building in great streams. My feet were starting to get cold, and the thought of returning to my dry bed sounded better with each additional minute. Maybe Fernando would come by later. But I knew I might miss my ride if I walked away. What would Daniel say if he knew I didn't go?

An hour later, a large cargo truck stopped in front of the market. He was going my way and for two dollars would take me. Three young women with long, dark hair pulled into ponytails climbed up the ladder after me. Knowing that I wasn't traveling alone made me relax a little. The vulnerability I felt as a woman in the world was raw and real even in the daylight. It was easy for Daniel to talk about adventure when, as a man, he moved through the world and this country with a level of safety I never had. Those beatnik adventurers Daniel admired were all white men like him. I loved being adventurous, seeing and doing new things, taking risks and having experiences no one I knew had ever experienced. But as a Native woman, I always had to think about safety and survival. I was scared, but didn't want to give anyone the satisfaction of letting my fear stop me. This required me to be hyperaware of my surroundings and especially of the men I encountered. My vigilance wouldn't protect me from everything, but it was the only way I knew how to live a life of adventure and not be paralyzed by fear.

The back of the truck, like most on the road, was a flatbed surrounded by walls of wood slats. A bus would have been better and safer, but sometimes a truck was the only way. I looked into the bed and was surprised to see that it was full of dirt. Dark, clumpy dirt. Six feet deep. I looked back at the other people waiting for rides. With their thin jackets and short skirts, they looked as cold as I felt. This might be my one and only chance to catch a ride today. At least this was safe. Dirty but safe. Once aboard, I exchanged a look with the girls. The tiny slip-on flats on their feet almost disappeared under the dirt. My thick-soled boots would keep me a few inches above it. I held on to the metal railing to steady myself. It was wet from the rain.

The driver banged on the side of the truck and honked an air horn to announce his departure. We passed the large brick school building across the street from the Children's Center. From this height, I could see the broken windows and holes in the chain-link fence. The white evangelical church inside the courtyard of the Children's Center stood empty. The truck approached the edge of town. Loose dogs walking slowly down the street sniffed once in our direction as we rumbled by. The houses were smaller and browner here. Eventually, there were no houses, only fields of flat, dry land.

One of the girls turned her head toward me and yelled something. All I heard was the gears shifting on the truck. I tucked my hair behind my ear and turned toward her.

"ABONO! Abono del cabra," she yelled and pointed down. I didn't know what she meant. *Cabra* meant goat. I furrowed my brow in confusion, and she pointed to her butt. Goat. Butt.

I was standing in goat shit. Goat fertilizer mixed with dirt. I had thought it was strange for a truck to transport dirt. As this sunk in, the rain came down harder. My hand slid around on the metal bar no matter how tightly I held on. My feet sunk down half an inch. I imagined myself continuing to sink until by the time the truck arrived, I would be a wet, shit-covered hand sticking out of the pile of fertilizer. The effort it took to hold on and not fall over made me sweat. I sniffed the air, but the only smell was the dirt and the diesel exhaust. The fertilizer must have been only a percentage of the mixture. I needed to believe that if I was going to survive.

The girls and I laughed about it together once the truck stopped and dropped us off. The little town where the anthropologist lived was not much bigger than Kantuta, and when I found my friends, I told everyone my story. The shit became stinkier and the rain colder with each retelling. My friends loved it. The anthropologist was happy I made the trek. She lent me a pair of her three-sizes-too-big jeans, which I was grateful to have because they were dry. We sat on the patio, sipping a cold beer and eating fajitas she had paid a cook to prepare. With a beer in my hand, a plate of warm food in front of me, and my friends around me, I relaxed my shoulders and appreciated the feeling of being there. The feeling of being in a room where I got the jokes and references, and where no one wondered what I was doing there. A room where I could disappear.

A few of us quietly left the larger party and headed to the hotel everyone was sharing. I was handed a mirror with several little white lines neatly arranged across it. Bolivian Marching Powder. Cocaine was cheap, high quality, and plentiful here in the central part of the country. We were only a day's drive from where the plants were grown and processed. The cavalier way volunteers bought and used cocaine made me nervous, and I had always avoided it. I never forgot that it was illegal. But sitting there, slightly buzzed from the beer and surviving another adventure, I decided not to pass up this opportunity. I did one long line and another when it came back around to me later.

Wow.

I felt like Wonder Woman after she spins around and stands there radiating power and beauty in her tiny star-spangled bustier. For someone who always felt as though she was doing everything wrong, this was a revelation. I was suddenly the smartest, sexiest, most confident version of me that ever existed. I was convinced that every single guy in the room wanted to get into my giant baggy pants, but none of them were good enough. I wanted to feel this way every day.

Then I remembered who I was. Anything that made me feel

this good could not be trusted. This could become a problem, especially here and now, where I usually drank to get through the horror of small talk. Coke presented a faster way to get to the social, talkative version of Ursula. But I had to walk away. I could never be a casual user. I spent the rest of the evening eating cold fajitas and drinking warm beer, listening to the anthropologist talk about goats. I made sure never to be in the room again when my friends were doing coke.

The next morning, my body felt like a bus that had run off the road and sat rusting at the bottom of a ravine. I was hungry but nauseated, and relieved when someone suggested we go to the market for fresh fruit *licuados* (smoothies). This town was smaller than Kantuta, but had the same white-painted mud houses and decades-old political graffiti on the walls. Shuffling along a few steps behind my four tall friends walking side by side, taking up the whole road, I followed them through the narrow cobblestone streets. As they passed a bag of coca leaves between them, it was clear that they never changed their behavior to fit into Bolivian society. A lifetime of adapting to the rules of the dominant society in the United States had taught me to watch and mimic how people dressed or spoke, and I had used that skill in Bolivia to conform. My friends a few steps ahead of me didn't. They did whatever they wanted, making no attempt to comport themselves to reflect Bolivian norms. Maybe I was the stupid one for attempting to dress or act like the Bolivians. But it was the only way I knew how to survive. I made it through training by watching the other volunteers for cues about how to act. When I was around other volunteers like this, I often had the feeling of not wanting to be associated with them, but not knowing exactly why. Yet I shared more with these powerful, embarrassing, wealthy people than with any of the

Bolivians. I stepped to the other side of the street and quietly sipped my licuado, watching the Bolivians watch my friends.

I was too debilitated to say good-bye to the anthropologist before catching the bus back to Kantuta. She was the first of what was to become an onslaught of departures. Friends I cared about, people who annoyed me, guys I had crushes on, and everyone else was about to leave.

16

La Flota — The Bus

Fernando kept visiting me. Sometimes he was there three times a week, and other times I wouldn't see him for two weeks. I had no idea when he was going to show up. He knocked on the heavy red door quietly, and I would let him in. The guilt I felt about the affair meant that I didn't want to ask him for anything. The inconsistency made it easier to convince myself that whatever we had wasn't serious; but our relationship, whatever it was, kept me from feeling lonely.

"I have to leave soon," he said to me one night. He didn't usually explain why he was leaving , and I never asked. For the first time, I wanted him to stay. I reached my arm across his chest and tucked my thumb into his armpit, grasping his round shoulder tighter.

"What did you think of me the night we left the party together?" I asked him.

"I was scared," he said. I laughed.

"Of me?" That was funny, because I had been scared of him.

"You hear things about girls from the States. I didn't know what to expect." He ran his hand along the outside of my arm.

"Am I different than Bolivian women?" I asked.

"No. Some are…like you." His hesitant response told me he didn't want to talk about this. Maybe this line of questioning made him uncomfortable; maybe he thought I was prying into his life. I was curious, but decided to drop the subject.

He cleared his throat. "We should go to Cochabamba." He explained a somewhat convoluted plan to secretly buy tickets and ride the bus together. I didn't understand why we couldn't walk up to the counter and buy tickets. Then I remembered how small Kantuta was. And I remembered his wife. I had forgotten about her. I assumed he was miserable. Why else did he keep coming back? But this conversation reminded me that there was someone else involved with this situation. That was between him and her. I was not cheating on anyone. I was an innocent bystander. That's what I told myself.

The thought of being together out in the open, walking around the city, holding hands, was tempting. We could go to a nice restaurant on the Prado, and maybe I could introduce him to my friends who lived in town. Before he left, we decided on a weekend to leave town together. I couldn't tell anyone, not Daniel and certainly not Teresa, because I knew they would try to talk me out of it. The secrecy of it was thrilling.

The day before I was supposed to sneak off to Cochabamba with Fernando, I went to Teresa's house after work to get my hair cut and colored. It was an excuse to hang out with the woman who was my best friend in town. She sat me down in the metal chair in the center of her packed-dirt patio. On weekends, Teresa and her brothers were building the house around them. Each time I visited, there were fewer exposed beams and more walls. Weekends were also when Teresa and her mother baked pastries to sell at the market. I was grateful that Teresa had time to cut my hair, even if I had to come over on a weekday after work.

"Who gave you *that?*" she asked, pointing to an ugly purple bruise on my neck. Fernando left a hickey on my neck a few nights before. I didn't realize until the next day that it was there. Had he given it to me on purpose like some junior high boy marking his territory? No one had mentioned it all day, and I thought no one had seen it.

"I don't remember," I said. This was a stupid answer, but all I could come up with in the moment. She had not asked me about Fernando before, and I hadn't told her anything. I knew I would eventually tell her. But I was trying to see whether she had heard anything around town. Sometimes I heard his name whispered, a little too loudly, on the street as I walked by a crowd of boys.

"So, you don't remember?" she asked as she moved around my head, snipping off the split ends. Maybe she really didn't know, or maybe she was playing with me. I couldn't tell. I set out the box of Señorita Clairol I bought during my last trip to Cochabamba. A shade darker than normal. She applied the dark, drippy mixture. The ammonia smell reminded me of home, of helping my mother color her hair. To be honest, I was bursting to tell Teresa about Fernando. My Peace Corps friends in other parts of the country knew, but to them it was a funny story. They didn't know him or his family. The situation fit into a stereotypical idea about the looser definition of monogamy we thought Latinos had. We assumed adultery was accepted here. I assumed it was not important.

"Fernando," I said as Teresa finished applying all the color. Maybe it wouldn't be a big deal to Teresa. She might scold me, but eventually we would be giggling about it the way we did when talking about the other guys in town.

"Fernando. Which Fernando? The fat guy who sells chickens near the mayor's office?" she asked. She put down the bowl of color and brush in her hand.

"No, I don't think he sells chickens, and he isn't fat." Was she teasing me? I couldn't tell whether she was pretending. I did not know enough details about him to give her much information. It wasn't until I told her that we'd met at a party that recognition flickered in her eyes. Maybe she actually hadn't known.

"Isn't he married to…," she started to ask and then covered her mouth. I nodded yes. This wasn't turning out as I had imagined it would. I started to sweat.

"Ursula, what are you doing with a married man?" She sat down in front of me and looked me straight in the eye. I shrugged my shoulders and squirmed under her gaze. What had I thought she would do? Give me a high five? Not exactly, but I hadn't expected this response.

"He has two children." I nodded my head yes. "Isn't his wife pregnant?" she asked. Pregnant? I hadn't known. His life beyond my bedroom was a mystery to me, and I preferred to stay in the dark. I tried to remember whether she'd been obviously pregnant.

"No…no tenia ningun idea." I tried to put as many negatives as I could in the sentence to make it clear that I didn't know. I closed my eyes and wanted to lie down, but knew that the dye in my hair was going to stain anything it touched. My scalp was warming up. I wanted her to rinse out the dye. Rinse it away down the sink. This was starting to sound like a telenovela. This was not supposed to happen to me. Teresa pulled the plastic gloves on and led me back to her patio where the sink was. She tipped my head down and ran the cold water. The warm sensation on my scalp ceased. Her brother walked in, and I was grateful because we had to stop talking about the subject. She styled my hair with a comb. Then she held up a small hand mirror for me to admire my new cut and color. The last thing I wanted was to look at my face in the mirror. But I did. My newly darkened hair looked great, but I felt terrible. I thanked her. We hugged good-bye, and she whispered in my ear that we should talk more later. Much later, in my opinion.

Halfway home I recovered from her response and realized I was angry. Angry at him for not telling me. Although I wasn't sure how he could have delivered that news. *Hey baby, thanks for the screw. FYI, my wife is pregnant. Again.* I was angry because this added a whole new layer to his betrayal. A man who cheats on his pregnant wife was pretty low. What did that make me?

And I was jealous. The bubbling darkness of jealousy surprised me. Of course, that was ridiculous, and I had no right to be jealous. But there it was. I was jealous of his wife. As I stomped through town with my dark, wet hair, all this churned in my brain.

Then I remembered the bus trip. Most likely I would not see him again until we were on the bus. The tickets were bought. I decided it was going to be our farewell trip, because this thing had suddenly become way more than I wanted.

It was Friday night, and half the town of Kantuta was standing outside the nightly bus bound for Cochabamba. Every evening around seven, a bus left from the corner down the street from my apartment, loaded with people and supplies. Women from the market pushed up against skinny kids saying good-bye to their fathers. Mothers hugged their adult children traveling to the city to look for work. This local bus was the main transportation for people traveling between Kantuta and the larger world.

The bus was a beat-up version of a Greyhound. The outside was yellowish brown like the hills outside Kantuta in the dry season. The employees of Flota Kantuta lifted heavy bags onto the roof. With thick rope and rubber straps, they tied everything to the top. The passengers climbed the steep steps, and, side-stepping down the narrow aisle with their blankets and bags, they found their assigned seat. Before the bus departed, passengers often slid open the windows and talked to people standing on the street. Arms and torsos reached out from inside, squeezing hands, grabbing small plastic bags of food, and passing money. The noise of the driver yelling at the employees on the roof, the good-byes, and the last-minute instructions made for a loud jumble. I was still hiding in my room, but I could imagine all this because it happened every time I rode the bus. Two or three times a month, I was right there with them, settling in for a long night.

I waited until the last possible moment to leave my apartment. I did not want any drama. The door shut behind me with a click, and I exhaled before stepping into the street. My hands were cold but sweating. Maybe his wife wouldn't be there, I hoped. Maybe he'd be on the bus alone. I slowly and deliberately crossed the uneven cobblestone street. The roar of the engine turning over let me know that the driver would be pulling out soon. No matter what happened, this was going to be over.

As I approached the bus, I sighed with relief because I did not see her. Or him. I wondered for half a second whether maybe he had decided not to make the trip. It would not be the first time he had made a promise that he didn't keep. There had already been nights when he had promised to visit and never showed up. I accepted it as the nature of the relationship. I was beginning to realize that married men made shitty boyfriends. The few days that had passed since I found out his wife was pregnant had somewhat cooled my anger toward him, but I still felt a slow burn of betrayal.

Keeping my head down, I stepped onto the bus and walked down the narrow aisle. There he was. Sitting by the window and looking out at the crowd. The light inside the bus was on, causing my reflection to appear in the glass. Just for a moment, I saw myself clearly as the rumpled hippy girl. The person reflected back was clearly not Bolivian. I was an outsider. Fernando turned his head toward me, and I stepped to the side. He looked back out the window. Then I noticed her. His wife.

Oh shit.

She was standing on the sidewalk under the streetlight with her face turned toward him. Her dark hair hung neatly around her shoulders. Her eyes were shadowed by the harsh streetlight, but I remembered their almond shape and striking darkness. Her form-fitting sweater and skirt revealed a curvy figure. With my oversized plaid shirt and rumpled khaki pants, I looked like a logger coming home from work. As was my habit, I preferred bulky, comfortable clothes. My mother taught me to see clothes as a utility, something to keep us warm that should have a lot of pockets. She worked in the forests of the Pacific Northwest, and although she was beautiful, with long black hair and smooth skin like some male fantasy of Pocahontas, she only wore Forest Service green or jeans with boots. There were few other Native Americans working in timber management, and for her to be taken seriously, to be given opportunities to advance, required her to wear regalia of a different type.

His wife was prettier than I remembered. Standing there demurely, with her hands at her sides, she could be any woman from any country. She was not a cholita wearing traditional dress and long braids. If she had been a cholita, I might have felt guiltier about this affair. The betrayal of an Indian woman by an Indian woman. I knew she was no less Indian because of her polyester skirt and bobbed haircut, but I didn't feel as guilty about the affair. Was that the swell of her pregnant belly under her shirt? Except for the one time she brought my laundry in from the rain, I had never spoken with her. I never would have thought that she and I would share something so intimate. Share someone. Was there was still time to run away?

My cheeks flushed. I waited for her expression to harden. It didn't. I waited for her to run onto the bus, wave her arms in the air, and call me a *puta*. She didn't. A large man pushed by me, and I saw the driver sit down behind the wheel. This was almost over. While holding my ticket in my hand, I looked down and then up at the number. I was pretending to look for my seat.

"Excuse me, sir, I think this is my seat." Fernando nodded. I hoped my act was fooling somebody. I reached up and placed my backpack on the rack above, but did not look at him. My armpits were wet with sweat. I plopped down in the hard seat and immediately smelled his cologne. His cheap sweet cologne that reminded me of the pressure of his body on top of me in my room. Of the tender but firm way he held my arms above my head last week when we were making love. His thigh was an inch from mine, but I couldn't touch him. My heart was ready to burst out of my chest, sprout legs, and run down the street. I pressed my lips together to keep from grinning. This was nerve-wracking. And fun.

The couple across from us talked to each other in Quechua. The greasy smell of fried chicken from the woman behind us made me slightly nauseous. The knot in my stomach grew larger and tighter. I knew his wife had seen me, seen us sitting together. Even if she did not know about our relationship, she knew me. I was still the woman who danced all night with her husband at a party. I wanted the bus to take off, to get moving.

HONK! I jumped. This was the driver's signal to everyone that he was getting ready to leave. He revved the engine and pulled the door shut, and the bus lurched forward. We turned the corner onto the main road to Cochabamba. I exhaled. In the dark spot between our seats, Fernando placed his hand in mine. It was warm and damp, like mine. I thought of him as an accomplished ladies' man who must have had hundreds of affairs. But in moments like this, I realized that he was like me, just a twenty-something trying to hide this romance.

Through the enormous windshield, Kantuta slid by. Both sides of the street were lined with the simple, flat exteriors common to most of the homes and businesses. A door or maybe a window out-lined in white paint was all that adorned the structures. No matter how beautiful the inside of a home was, the outsides looked very similar and plain. Groups of teenage boys slunk down the sidewalk toward the main plaza. At a bar, wide-open doors revealed men sitting at simple wood tables with their arms raised requesting more beer. Outside the bar, a young woman fried small hot dogs in her portable food cart while her one-year-old baby girl played on the sidewalk. We passed the bank building with its ornate black metal window gates, closed and dark now. The butcher was pulling down the heavy metal door at the *carniceria* and going home for the night. An older woman sitting on the curb outside an open door waved at the bus as it passed. Once we passed the bridge on the far end of town and the last street lamp, the driver pressed on the accelerator, and the bus sped on into the night.

I grew up riding buses in the US, taking Greyhound and Trailways everywhere I wanted to go. Portland to San Francisco to visit my grandparents. Washington, DC, to San Francisco after attending a political rally. Portland to New Orleans to LA and back to Portland, visiting friends along the way. During my teens and early twenties, any extra money went toward a bus ticket somewhere. The sound of the air brakes, the rumble under the seats of the motor, even the chemical stench drifting out of the bathroom always made me sit up straight and buzz with anticipation. The bus meant freedom and a kind of achievable adventure. Freedom from the small, damp towns of the Pacific Northwest where my mother's search for a good job took us. They were beautiful towns with forests and mountains, but I was curious about what else was out there in the world.

The bus also meant anonymity. I did not have to explain who I was, who my family was, where I was from. All that mattered was where I was headed. Even on this bus, there were some faces I recognized and probably more who knew me as one of the three gringos living in town. Like passengers on buses everywhere, people kept to themselves even when they knew each other. Now here I was in this little seat, pushed up against Fernando, knowing that we couldn't move for several hours. I smiled at him in the light. He smiled back, and I noticed the gold-rimmed tooth that I used to think looked cheap. Now I loved it. I was still angry at him, but the excitement of the departure and what awaited us in town made me willing to skip the breakup part until the end of the trip.

The bus pulled into Cochabamba before dawn. The station was a few blocks from the big outdoor market where vendors sold everything from underwear to spices. Across the street was a low metal gate with spikes at the top. Except for two old taxis and an old car being loaded with someone's bag, the streets were empty. About half of the passengers stayed on. It was too early for the minivans that served as public transportation to take them into the city. Fernando and I stood several feet away from each other on the street outside. Fetid water pooled in a pothole near the corner, and a skinny dog dug in a pile of trash.

Because I took this bus every couple of weeks, I had been at this exact spot many times. The first time I arrived, the darkness and unfamiliarity frightened me, and I didn't get off the bus until the sun came up. Riding the bus with Fernando made this arrival seem easy. Eighteen months of living in Bolivia had taught me to adopt my tough-woman-traveler posture in situations like this. I knew to assess the street ahead of me to avoid rabid dogs, drunks looking to get laid, and taxi drivers charging me twice the normal price. Having someone to help me get from here to the apartment in town that I shared with other volunteers was a relief. I motioned toward a waiting taxi and jumped into the back. Fernando slipped in beside me. The driver looked back at us in the rearview mirror as he sped off toward the city. I held my breath until we were out of sight of the bus.

"Can you let me in?" I said into the speaker of the apartment building. I knew the other volunteers were awake because, even three stories down, I could hear them. Fernando stood behind me on the street. A dog barked in the distance. Buzz. I pushed open the black gate and walked inside. Our feet echoed against the tile floor as Fernando followed me up three flights of barely lit stairs toward the roof. I slowly pushed open the heavy metal door. My two worlds were about to come face-to-face. Fernando was about to meet my volunteer friends. I wondered whether he thought it strange that I shared a two-bedroom apartment with three men. The apartment was our crash pad, a filthy place that several volunteers and the occasional US or European expat shared. The apartment provided the perfect place to sleep, hook up, party, and recuperate from hangovers. Everyone chipped in on the rent and brought plates and cups, although I was the only one to buy toilet paper on a regular basis.

We emerged onto the rooftop patio. The patio was littered with beer bottles and nearly empty green bags of coca. As Chris, Jake, and Tom chewed on the dry leaves, their jaws clenched and unclenched. Each guy gave me a fermented hug. All three of them were taller than I by a head. Darkened rooftops with pointy television antennae and giant cement water tanks spread out for miles. Half-finished apartment buildings and the backside of a centuries-old church stood above the smaller buildings. I couldn't see the stars as I could in Kantuta.

"This is Fernando." One of the guys raised his eyebrow, curious about this Bolivian arriving in the middle of the night with me. I had told them about Fernando, but they didn't remember. It was unusual to bring Bolivians into one of our crash pads. These overpriced apartments were the places where we re-created US life as best we could. Here we didn't have to project the best version of ourselves. Still, if the guys could have found a way to surreptitiously high five me at that moment, they would have. Getting together with hot Bolivians was sport for volunteers. The resulting hookups could be called conquests. I hadn't thought of Fernando that way, but standing here with my friends, I wanted them to think my relationship with Fernando was an uncomplicated notch on my belt.

Each of the guys shook Fernando's hand and offered him a warm beer. He graciously refused them. I was glad because I was exhausted and only wanted to sleep. I pulled Fernando into one of the open bedrooms, and we slipped under a heavy blanket on an unmade bed. Fernando asked me several questions about the volunteers, wondering where the guys lived. Was he impressed by this patio full of drunk white men? I couldn't keep my eyes open. I answered him and then fell asleep.

The sun shining through the window woke me the next morning. There was nothing in this room but a mattress on the floor and backpacks piled in corners. Nothing on the walls, not even curtains over the windows. Fernando was sleeping. It was the first time I had ever seen him sleep. He always left my apartment in Kantuta in the middle of the night. But here he was, taking up half the bed like a real boyfriend. There, I'd done it again—I'd thought of him as my boyfriend. Was that what he was? He looked sweet and harmless as he breathed in and out.

I wanted to ask him about his wife, ask whether it was true that she was pregnant. But as I thought about what words to use, how to say it in Spanish, I wondered if it was my business. Maybe I didn't have the right to dig into every corner of his life. I didn't think he had the right to every nook of my personal life. This mistress situation was strange. I didn't know how to act.

"I heard something about you," I said almost as soon as I noticed he was awake. I rolled over and looked him in the eye. My stomach tightened. I hated confrontation, but I knew I had to say something.

"Sí?" he said, taking my hand and placing it against his chest.

"Your wife," I said slowly. It was not a term I ever expected to say to him. He was awake now. "Is she pregnant?" Maybe if I had more of a grasp of Spanish, I could soften what I was saying, make it easier, less confrontational. Big words had always been like armor to me. In a world where I never felt that I had much power or privilege, I used carefully crafted sentences with SAT-worthy words to protect myself. Here in Bolivia that was not an option. I could order a drink at a bar, but emotional conversations were another thing. He cleared his throat.

"Yes," he brought my hand to his lips and kissed it. He was silent for a while as he watched my face.

"And?" I said.

"I thought you already knew; that night at the party everyone was talking about it." It made me uncomfortable to hear anything about their relationship, forcing me to see him as more than simply a hot guy fulfilling my personal need for intimacy and affection. He was a husband and a father.

"Don't you feel any guilt about this?" I asked. I wasn't trying to shame him. I genuinely wondered. And if he didn't feel guilty, then maybe I didn't have to feel guilty either. He pulled away and started to get up. His look hardened, and for the first time, he seemed angry.

"Look, I'm sorry," I sat up. "I don't have the right to ask you that. I don't know if we should do this anymore." Even as I said the words, I felt conflicted. Did I really want to end this? Daniel was about to leave for the States, and I still had several months left in Kantuta. I did not want to spend that time alone. I had my friendship with Teresa, but I knew what my nights would be like.

"We're here now; let's enjoy this weekend and talk about it back in Kantuta," he said. I exhaled. I was chickening out. I should have ended it. But I wasn't going to do that. I did not have the courage to end it. I dressed quickly and headed out the door, not wanting to talk to anyone about anything. I wanted to distract myself with the mundane task of finding food.

After mango smoothies in the market, we rode a bus to a small community on the outskirts of town. He held my hand as we walked down narrow cobblestone streets and around the main plaza. To me, the plaza, the streets all looked like those in any of the many small towns I had visited while in Bolivia. But something about walking around freely without worrying that anyone we knew might see us made them exciting and interesting. Fernando crossed the street to ask a man for a restaurant suggestion. I watched him talk to the man in the mix of Spanish and Quechua that I almost understood. He stroked his chin as he looked in the direction that the man was motioning. I forgot sometimes, but seeing him on the street like this reminded me how gorgeous he was. Knowing that he was with me and all mine even for a few hours was thrilling.

Was his brownness part of his appeal? Not only his skin color but his Indianness. He was both familiar and exotic to me. After the interaction with the other volunteers on the patio, I wondered whether that played any part in my attraction to him. In the past, non-Native boyfriends sometimes told me how "cool" it was that I was an American Indian. Highlighting my identity never made me feel cool. I usually thought, *Wait, is that what you like about me? What about my sparkling personality? My understanding of Marx's theory of exploitation?* I never told Fernando that I loved his brownness, because it sounded like something a clueless white person would say, but I thought it. Fernando was undeniably Indigenous. People called him Indio. Indian. In Bolivia, that was an insult. Couldn't an olive-skinned girl get hot and bothered about the brownness of her lover without its being exoticism? Loving his brownness was part of my growing appreciation of my own.

I followed Fernando to a bar, where he ordered a pitcher of *guarapo*, the sweet grape liqueur famous in that area. He seemed to enjoy taking command of the situation and paid for everything before I could find my wallet. On the table was a cup with five dice for cacho. Fernando played like a Bolivian, meaning that he was smooth and quick and won every round. A Yahtzee fan from my youth, I usually held my own when playing with other volunteers, but I was no match for this man who had been playing the game his whole life.

"What do we call each other? You and I," I asked. Not that I would have a chance to describe our relationship to anyone, but I was curious because I had started to think of him as my boyfriend. "Amantes? Amores?" I suggested.

"No." He pulled back, looking at me as if to say that those words were dirty and insufficient.

"Somos novios." He kissed me. I wanted to ask Teresa or Ximenita what the difference between terms was, but knew that wasn't possible without a lot of questions. The words *novios* and *amantes* had always been synonyms on the glossary page of Spanish textbooks. I suspected that *novios* meant something more. I would continue to think of him as my boyfriend.

The waiter kept his eyes on me for an extra moment. I wanted to think that the two of us looked like a regular Bolivian couple out for a Saturday afternoon trip. But that extra second of attention from the waiter made me think we couldn't even fool this complete stranger.

Fernando was returning to Kantuta by himself that night. As crazy and rushed as that seemed to me, people from Kantuta took quick day trips like this all the time.

"The next time, we should stay the night," he said. We kissed good-bye outside the hideous cement-and-steel building on a choked and polluted street that was the Cochabamba bus station. I took a taxi back to the apartment. Without my Bolivian escort, I was once again a woman alone in a big city. A tourist had recently been raped on the hill a few blocks behind the station, and it was big news because Cochabamba had a reputation for safety. Even amid the discarded garbage and people beat down by an economy that offered them few opportunities, I loved Cochabamba. The cab passed by a hidden plaza full of kids practicing for a parade and the one nameless store I loved that sold lotions and perfumes like a misplaced Bath & Body Works. I was exhausted by the drama of the trip, by speaking only in Spanish all day and night, by getting little sleep, and by wondering whether Fernando was a good guy.

17

Cantando — Singing

Daniel's despedida was being held near where he had helped get the wells installed. There were only a few farmers' houses and, as I discovered when I arrived, a newly built school and basketball court. Daniel had collected donations from his parents' church back in California to pay for the supplies, but the farmers and their families had built all of it. The school was simple, containing only desks and chairs, but it was a school where none had previously been. The basketball court was a flat cement square with a hoop. But spaces like this in rural communities represented more than places to play basketball. The school and court would become a gathering spot.

Someone handed a battery-operated microphone to the mayor, and he went on and on about Daniel. It was sweet. They presented him with a vest made from a goat in the community. It was stiff and barely fit his broad shoulders, but I saw him wipe his eyes as they helped him put it on. His Spanish had improved a little since that first ch'alla I attended with him a year and a half earlier—but not much. Still, he was funny and sincere. Then the mayor shook his hand and rubbed confetti in his hair. The connection Daniel had with the people in the community seemed genuine. Did the real value of the Peace Corps lie in changing people through connection? Who was changing more—those of us from the US or the Bolivians? Maybe we were simply glorified exchange students, humanizing each other one bucket of chicha at a time.

I shook my head. I was trying too hard to find meaning in this moment. I wanted to believe that what I was seeing was a good thing. That it wasn't simply the Western world telling the Bolivians what they needed. It wasn't that, but I wasn't sure what it was.

By the next night, everyone was gone. Daniel packed up the few belongings he hadn't already sent, and we got two seats side by side on the Flota Kantuta. I knew this would cause gossiping about us, but I didn't care. Fernando had stopped asking about my friendship with Daniel, but I knew he was not comfortable with my spending so much time alone with another man. Outside the window, it was dark except for the outline of the mountains illuminated by the moonlight. Graduate school, surfing, and beautiful California women—Daniel had a long list of things he was looking forward to. The future seemed bright for him. I envied it. My departure would not be so neat.

"What does Fernando's house look like?" I asked. It was dark outside the window, and we couldn't see the farms or roads that we knew were there. Daniel and Fernando had become friends in the last few months, which surprised and pleased me. I didn't even know exactly where Fernando's house was. That was on purpose. I stayed away from that side of town. Daniel made sure to mention Fernando's wife and his children in the description.

"You have got to drop that dude," Daniel finally said. "He's cool and everything, but he's using you."

"Maybe you're right, but he gives me something I need," I said. I shifted in my seat. It was so dark I couldn't see his face.

"It isn't because he's married; well, maybe it is a little bit, but really," he scratched his chin. "You deserve someone who treats you better." I had tried to hide all the ways I had curtailed my life because of the affair. But Daniel saw them. The nights when I hurried back to my room, saying I was tired but really wanting to be home in case Fernando stopped by.

"You probably should watch how much you're drinking," he said. I turned my head because I couldn't believe that Mr. Cocktails before Noon was telling me not to drink so much. "Your people, you know, sometimes have problems with drinking."

"What?" I said as calmly as I could. Was he calling me a drunk Indian?

"I'm not saying you do, but I worry about you sometimes."

I shook my head but said nothing. He liked to do this—act as though he knew things I didn't, and it always annoyed me. I was angry but not surprised. This was the risk I took whenever I let people know I was Native. It reminded me of how even my friends saw me. They might love knowing a real Native, but when they saw me with a drink in my hand, they remembered the stereotype. I might have had a problem with drinking, but it wasn't because I was Native.

He was silent after that, and I shifted away. In Cochabamba the next morning, we said our good-byes standing on the wide, flat sidewalk in the shadow of a church spire. He kissed me on the cheek, and I knew I would cry if I said anything. I wondered what Kantuta would be like without him.

Soon after, I moved into a smaller apartment in the same house. There was a tiny room, painted bright pink, with a separate door that opened to a side street. I was tired of having to sneak around my own house, listening for a knock in the middle of the night. I used to live on the second floor in a big room with large windows; now I was in a small room with one window that faced inside to the courtyard. I was choosing privacy over a view of the world.

Lying in my bed one morning, I realized that my period was late. I didn't want to be pregnant, but I hadn't been acting like it. The small bag of multicolored condoms I gathered from the medical office sat mostly undisturbed in the corner of my mosquito net. The medical officer gave every volunteer bags of free condoms and made us promise to use them. With Fernando, it was a battle that I waged each time we were together. Sometimes I won; sometimes I didn't.

Safe sex had been an obsession in college. I was determined not to get pregnant. The child of a young single mother, I saw the judgments made of my mother, and I was not going to follow in her footsteps. Finishing high school and enrolling in college was my path out. No high school boyfriends, no make-out sessions in the backseat of my Corolla, and no fumbling with button flies on the couch after everyone at the party was asleep. When I finally had a boyfriend, I made him wear three condoms at once. Well, not really, but I would have if that was what the situation required. During my sophomore year of college, my best friend's partner tested positive for HIV, which scared me.

So why didn't I force Fernando to wear a condom every time? I knew better. But I was tired of being so damn good. Tired of ignoring what I wanted to do and always following the rules in order to survive. Tired of trying to make the absolute smartest choice about everything. I went to college while the other twenty-somethings in my family were in and out of jail and my sister lived on the street. From the outside, it looked as though I knew how to make smart choices. But I was struggling, and I didn't trust myself. My choices were based on what I thought would look good and smart to other people. I excelled at ignoring my impulses. Denying myself the things I craved was part of my survival plan. Until now.

Unprotected sex with a married man was stupid times stupid. I knew that. But sometimes stupid felt like rebellion. Rebellion against the narrow path that I was expected to follow. What better place to loosen the reins I had pulled tight my whole life than here where I experienced power and privilege that I didn't have in the United States? My behavior seemed to be without consequences. I wondered if I could even get pregnant.

"Oh, our babies will be so beautiful," he whispered in my ear some nights, and I allowed myself to be seduced. He promised everything forever, and it sounded good. Never had a man promised me anything beyond a semester. Although life with Fernando might come with problems, I thought it would be better than a life alone, a future that seemed likely on dark days. He kept asking about returning with me to the States. I stopped trying to convince him that he would hate the US. I didn't even know where I would find a job after I returned home, and the thought of supporting someone who didn't speak English or know the culture seemed beyond me.

The Children's Center became a refuge for me. One afternoon, little Tomas brought me a deck of cards. We decided to play Concentration, the game of matching and memory. He helped me lay all the cards face down in neat rows on a table. Tomas didn't say much during the first few rounds. This wasn't unusual—he was a quiet kid. I didn't know whether he had played the game before or understood how to play it. But by the fourth game, he was making more matches than I was, and I could tell he had it. He won the next game. Other children joined us, and as each one came up, Tomas explained the rules. Soon there were four kids at our table. Tomas laughed, and I noticed him mumbling to himself while he decided which cards to pick up. Never had I seen him so open and comfortable. When I saw Tomas thriving, I felt better about being at the Center. Despite the complex morality of a Third World children's home supported by wealthy Westerners and the Center's limited resources, kids like Tomas and Umberto were surviving, in part, because of the Center.

The days at the Center now had a predictable rhythm. I would help in the kitchen in the morning if they needed it, and as long as they weren't serving *tripa*, I always ate lunch with the children. When I sat with the little kids, such as Tomas and Umberto, I asked them about their favorite type of food (*manzanas*) or what words they knew in English (hamburger). With Celia and the other teenage girls, we talked about boys and family. The teenage boys I met in the charango workshop asked me about the United States. In the afternoon, I helped with their English homework. Their textbooks were falling apart, and they were being taught a version of

English spoken by no one I knew. English pronunciation was difficult for them with all of the strange rules. A boy asked me how to say "Sioux City, Iowa," and it took me a moment to remember. I rarely thought about the bigger picture anymore, about economic development and how the world should be remade. I was content to simply live my life.

I made the mistake of telling Simon at the Children's Center about the new court Daniel had helped get built. He asked me if I could find funds to pay for a court at the Center. This wasn't the first time I had heard this request, but it upset me. Every week, it seemed, someone was asking me to help pay for a project. A woman down the street approached me all the time about her plan to build a school for blind children and asked if I could help fund it. I changed the route I took to work to avoid her. Never did anyone ask me to help plan these projects. I thought about all the times I whipped out the equivalent of $100 and paid for flour for a project without giving it a second thought. Did that make them think I had an endless supply of money? I hated to tell them, but I had no idea where to get money for their projects. There were small grants from Peace Corps, but I wasn't sure how to apply for them. Daniel's parents helped him raise money through their church back in California. This wasn't an option for me.

Simon informed everyone during breakfast that we would be walking in the Independence Day parade through the center of Kantuta. August 6 was Independence Day across Bolivia, and to celebrate almost two hundred years as an independent country, Kantuta would have a parade. Simon held up a picture of what the children were expected to wear, ironed slacks and a clean collared shirt for the boys, a skirt and blouse for the girls. If they didn't have these items, they could come and watch, but wouldn't be marching.

"You, too, señorita," the director said as he walked past me. "Skirt, skirt, remember to wear a skirt." He wasn't letting me decide what might look nice. I was surprised that he invited me to march with all the teachers and students. Maybe he finally saw me as a legitimate part of the Children's Center. I owned only one skirt, but it was too long and flowy to wear in a parade. In the clothing store near the house I rented, I found a thin polyester blouse, black skirt, and flats. I wasn't sure they would last more than a few months, but by then I would be gone. It was the first time I had bought clothes outside of the overpriced alpaca sweaters every non-Bolivian buys while in La Paz.

On the bright, clear morning of August 6, I walked into the Children's Center wearing my new outfit. I was nervous because I appeared to be trying to look Bolivian but not quite getting it right. Ximenita walked around me, inspecting my skirt, shoes, and blouse. She clucked her tongue approvingly and raised her eyebrows up and down Groucho Marx style. We laughed. Ximenita's teasing always put me at ease.

"Listo?" the director asked. "Ladies and gentlemen, it is time to march." Twenty kids in clean button-up shirts or blouses, pants or skirts, and shined shoes came out of the cafeteria and followed the director to the main square a few blocks away. Tomas waved from the side of the road where he and Umberto stood in white school smocks and sandals. They looked relieved not to be marching. The Center's flags were unfurled, and we waited on a side street until it was our turn. It wasn't until we were given our go-ahead that I realized the whole town was there. The main plaza was lined with families and children watching each group march. None of the marchers were smiling and waving, only looking straight ahead expressionless like soldiers. Teresa, Ximenita, Florencia, and all the kids were serious. I pressed my lips together to keep from smiling: I was loving it. I was a part of Kantuta, in a way that no tourist would be.

The plaza was small, and in a few minutes, we were marching past the mayor sitting on a stage near the courthouse. Once we were off the main plaza, the group dispersed and started laughing. I was the only person with a camera, and everyone asked me to take pictures of them. No one smiled when I took their pictures. I had long ago learned that Bolivians over the age of five rarely smiled in pictures. In my pictures, I am smiling broadly, my arms around the kids. I tucked my camera under my arm. I would have to get the film developed quickly if I was going to give them their pictures before leaving Kantuta. I hoped Fernando had seen me. I hoped the whole town had seen La Ursula marching with El Centro Infantil.

A group of new volunteers descended on Kantuta, all ten freshly arrived from the United States, at the start of their Peace Corps adventure. Luckily, I didn't have to entertain them, because I had important things to do, such as wait for Fernando to come over, write in my journal about how much I missed Fernando, and rejoice that I wasn't pregnant. I had dodged the baby bullet and decided it was time to find out whether my medical coverage included birth control pills.

The volunteers were from the group that replaced Daniel, and they spent the day with his engineer friends. I went to buy a pack of cigarettes at the pharmacy down the street and saw a tall white guy with a beard and sandals. He must be one of them.

"You Peace Corps?" I asked. He took a step back and seemed

surprised I was speaking English.

"Yeah, are you that other volunteer here?" That other volunteer. Even though Daniel had left Kantuta, I was still the other volunteer. He invited me to the restaurant where everyone was gathering for dinner. I couldn't say no.

"What's it like to be here?" a woman asked.

"You must have tons of great stories." Someone poured me a beer. I didn't normally enjoy playing the experienced volunteer role because I felt that I had to impress them. I couldn't talk about the things I was struggling with. Happy-go-lucky volunteer was the example they wanted. Daniel had been great at that, and I wished he were there right then.

"Well, there's this bakery project I started, which was cool. Although it kind of faded out after a while." None of them looked impressed.

"I can't wait to be at my site. These people, these Bolivians, are so beautiful, and I can't wait to help them." She was the kind of natural sandy-haired woman I knew well from years of working with peace-and-justice nonprofits in the United States. Honestly, we probably would have been good friends had we met before this. But in that moment, she was a clueless infant and I was a hundred years old. I had wandered so far off the path I had intended to follow that I could barely remember what I had imagined the volunteer experience would be. What I wanted to tell them was that Kantuta had become as exotic as Cleveland to me. I was living a normal boring life, trying to keep my socks clean, keep food on my kitchen shelves, and contribute something at my job.

Mercifully, they decided soon after that to walk over to a chicharia that the engineers had said was the best in town. It was good chicha, sweeter than it was sour, and we sat around a large wood table. We played cacho, and for once, I didn't lose. All those nights playing with and losing to Daniel had taught me how to play, how to bluff, and how to take a risk when I had nothing to lose. That old urge to play the tough, hard-drinking chick and the very real nervousness I felt around these fresh-faced volunteers were all the excuse I needed to drink more. I kept thinking I needed to leave and wait for Fernando, but my apartment was only a few blocks away, and it was still early.

"Hola, Ur," I felt on my neck more than I heard. It was Fernando. I looked around nervously. None of the people at the table knew or cared who he was. He sat down in the seat next to me, and I introduced him to the volunteers. The sandy-haired woman nodded approvingly in my direction, and I had to admit I was pleased. I passed around my cheap Bolivian cigarettes and we threw dice, then suddenly, Fernando was holding a guitar.

"Con dinero, sin dinero…" He began the first lines of a popular song even I knew because it played on the radio so frequently. The volunteers were drunk enough to think they knew it and sang along. I looked at my boyfriend strumming the guitar and the crowd cheering him on, and couldn't believe this was happening. He kissed me on the cheek as he finished the song. I blushed, but was enjoying the attention.

Then I had one drink too many and decided I was mad at Fernando. I asked him why he didn't come to see me more often and why I always had to wait for him. He laughed, but I continued pressing him, getting louder each time.

"Cállate," he whispered. He was telling me to shut up. Oh, now I was really mad.

"Take me home," I said in my best calm but angry voice. I was embarrassed that he'd tried to control me in front of the other volunteers. The sandy-haired woman would not meet my eyes.

I couldn't figure out how to put the keys into my door lock, so he opened it for me. I thought he would follow me into my mosquito net, but he left. The next morning, I cringed at my drunken behavior. I would never see any of those people again, but I hated that their last memory of me would be of a messy, drunk woman being told to shut up by her Bolivian boyfriend. I pulled the covers back over my head and wondered what I was doing with my life.

18

Bailando — Dancing

"Esta noche! Un gran fiesta con los mariachis de La Paz," blasted the loudspeaker on top of a dented sedan circling the streets. There was going to be a dance at the old market that evening. I had lived in Kantuta long enough to realize what a big deal a dance with a live band was. The man's voice jiggled as the car bounced over the cobblestone streets. The sound grew louder as they neared my house, then disappeared. It was a Thursday, and I had taken the day off to finish paperwork. The end of my service was as bureaucratic as the application process had been. The difficulty of summarizing what I had done for the last two years into a three-page document was that I ran out of things to say halfway down the first page. I could name few accomplishments that a Peace Corps official would consider valuable.

Started a bakery project with the girls—which ended when school was over for the year and everyone went home.

Made a charango—which sat on my table, gathering dust.

Tutored the kids with English homework—but because they were learning British English from a twenty-year-old textbook, half the time I did not know what their homework said.

Managed the development of a popsicle business—and by *manage*, I mean filled plastic bags with sugary purple liquid and stuck them into a freezer.

I described it all in a way that would impress a hiring manager in the United States, but it was tough. Of the projects I had worked on, the bakery project was the only one that felt like an accomplishment. It had allowed me to connect with Teresa and the girls at the Center. Yet when I heard about the large and small accomplishments of the other volunteers, my little bakery and popsicle business successes seemed minuscule.

Most difficult of all was how to put into words my disillusionment with the central conceit—the central assumption—behind many of the projects: develop projects that replicated businesses and organizations in the United States because that was the model to follow. Not every project made that assumption, and what Jodi had done at the girl's home and Daniel had done with the farmers seemed indisputably worthwhile. But too many projects were based less on what the Bolivians needed and more on what a volunteer could envision and pull off in two years. A volunteer once told me that his great idea was to create a store only open to members who paid a fee in exchange for lower prices.

"Sam's Club," he whispered in my ear. I laughed, but I wondered whether a discount warehouse was really what Bolivia needed to survive in the global economy. Given that most of us were fresh out of college with little knowledge or experience other than having grown up in the United States, what else did we have to offer?

The cholita who worked for my neighbor turned on the water

in the courtyard, and it reminded me to get back to my paperwork. Why was I wasting my time thinking about this? Who was I to think this? I was a girl who grew up eating free school lunches and graduated from a state university no one had ever heard of. What did I know about economic development? I was lucky to have been invited and, if that recruiter was to be believed, only given the chance because Peace Corps needed more minorities.

Yet maybe this was precisely why I noticed when projects seemed to embody this underlying assumption. I knew that the way things were done in the US was not always the right way. My perspective on this work was colored by the life I had lived through, the many Indian people I knew who suffered under legal and educational systems build on these same assumptions. "Do it like we do it and you'll be better off" was not true to me. I crossed out the last line of my report and put my head down on the table as the loudspeaker approached my street again. I needed a distraction. Two volunteers had recently moved to Kantuta to work in the communities where Daniel had been. I hadn't spent any time with them, but thought I should take them to the dance and teach them about life in Kantuta as Daniel had done for me.

Considering that I had one month left in Kantuta, this was likely to be my last dance at the market. I put on the white polyester blouse and black skirt I'd bought for the Bolivian Independence Day parade. The outline of my white camisole could be seen through the thin fabric, and the buttons hung by a single thread. I stepped in front of my full-length mirror and thought I looked almost Bolivian. My hair was shorter than most Bolivian women's. My dark hands stood out against the white blouse. Sometimes I'd press my hand against Fernando's bare chest and see that the darkest part of my body was the same color as the lightest part of his.

"Mucho gusto conocerte," I said to no one as crisply and perfectly as I could. Standing by the mirror, I stuck my hand out in front of me and pretended to shake someone's hand. I practiced standing demurely with my hands at my sides. I turned and looked at my profile. My thick middle was evident, the widest part of my apple-shaped body. My whole life I'd hated that apple shape. I even hated the word *apple* because it was a euphemism for *fat*. Two years in Bolivia had given me the tiniest bit of acceptance of my shape, of how the curves of my hip and my stomach were simply features of my unique body. In Bolivia, fat didn't mean ugly. Fat was just one body type. Some people were fat; others were skinny. Still, two years couldn't undo a lifetime of living in a culture where fat did mean ugly. I was about to return to my fat-obsessed culture, but I hoped I could carry some of this acceptance home with me.

My own grandfather had reminded me on a regular basis that losing weight was as simple as "eating less and exercising more." He'd silently shake his head and purse his lips when I emerged from the kitchen with a second glass of chocolate milk. I'd turn away from him and roll my eyes, but I accepted that he was right. As he was the only adult male in my life, it was hard not to think he spoke for all mankind. He was trying to help me understand the rules of the world as he understood them. During my teenage years, I argued with him about his archaic ideas of men's and women's roles, but when my jeans were too tight, I'd remember everything he'd said about eating and exercising.

Bolivian women were not free of weight-loss worries. I practiced my Spanish with Teresa by reading weight-loss articles in the newspaper. But not every woman from ten to ninety was obsessed with trying to get skinny. Hefty. Chunky. Big boned. All these words we had in English that kept us from saying the word *fat*. *Bien gordita* was a phrase more than one Bolivian man had used to describe me. I thought it meant something like "nice and chubby." Part of the reason I'd become less self-conscious about my weight was that the Bolivians weren't afraid to say the word. *Fat* became less powerful when it wasn't whispered or considered the worst thing for a woman to be. Food also was still connected to survival in Bolivia. Malnourishment was a very real problem, especially out in the countryside. A fat woman was a healthy woman.

I turned back around and faced myself in the mirror. I wasn't going to play Bolivian. I changed into a skirt I brought from the States. I knew how ridiculous non-Native people in fake Native American regalia looked. I did not want to be the gringa putting on the Bolivian outfit.

I led the two new volunteers under the high orange arch above the entrance into the old market. The young woman sitting behind the table smiled as I handed over three bolivianos. I could already hear the horns bouncing around the brick and adobe walls of the market. We walked down the dark alley and emerged into the open-air patio that shimmered with light, music, and movement. The two flat cement slabs in the center were lit up with strings of lights and transformed into dance floors. Five portly men in wide-brimmed mariachi hats and black suits blasted music to the crowd. The horns blared loudly and then the guitar and violin joined in. Playing fast with a lively beat, the men then leaned into each other and began singing in harmony. A song about midnight and love. Teenage couples in jeans and flats, grinning widely, swung each other energetically around the dance floor. An older gentleman in a collared shirt twirled a gray-haired woman. Leaning against a brick column smoking a cigarette was Johnny, the James Dean of Kantuta. He sometimes flirted with me but was still only a kid just out of high school, so I didn't encourage him.

Sitting at a small wood table was Ximenita. Even in her modest but form-fitting dress she was a knockout. I never understood why men were not flocking around her. Maybe because of her status as the dark-skinned cook's helper with no family or money. Ximenita and I had spent many hours together laughing and gossiping, and having her here made me feel a little more comfortable. We sat and talked until a doctor I had once been introduced to asked me to dance. His clammy white hand closed around mine, and he held me tightly. A little too tightly.

"I like your figure," he leaned in and whispered into my ear. I thanked him and pulled back a little. He was a little creepy, but harmless. He bought me a beer. When I rejoined Ximenita at her table, I asked where the new volunteers were. She told me they had left a few songs earlier.

"Are they together?" she asked.

"No, just friends. Like Daniel and I were." She rolled her eyes. She never believed Daniel and I were only friends.

"Do you miss him?" she asked.

"Claro que sí, muchisimo." Of course I missed him. But I thought I was figuring out how to survive in Kantuta by myself. Ximenita motioned with her chin toward the entrance and raised her eyebrows while looking at me. It was Fernando, slightly disheveled in an untucked shirt. He stared at me as he took a drag on a cigarette and walked in our direction.

"Oh, who is that?" I asked. I had to pretend. I knew people were gossiping about us because Teresa told me. Ximenita must have known. She watched me as he came closer, stumbling and drifting a little as he made his way toward me. Great, he was drunk.

"Hola, Urrr," he said when he reached our table. Ximenita covered her mouth to hold in a laugh. She loved gossip, and this was like finding an extra-tender slice of meat hidden in her soup. Having to pretend I didn't know him was a reminder of all the things we couldn't do. He stood close enough for me to smell his cheap cigarettes. I crossed my arms over my chest and pressed my lips together in an attempt to hide any evidence of a reaction.

"Vamos a bailar," he said. It was the exact phrase he'd used the night I met him. How many months ago had that been? Back then, it sounded brave and enticing. Now it seemed to be less an invitation and more of a command. He stumbled off to another table. I smirked at Ximenita as though he was simply another drunk flirt. I should have left. I knew nothing good could come of this. But it was my last dance at the market. Instead of leaving, I drank another beer. I wanted to be out on the dance floor.

"Quieres bailar?" he asked. I'd been trying to ignore him for three dances. The self-righteous angry girlfriend was a role I loved to play. I knew being seen together might confirm the rumors. But I couldn't stop myself. I placed my hand in his and let him lead me. He swung me out and pulled me toward him. He held me close, closer than an unmarried woman and a married man should be dancing. His hand pressed on my lower back, and I curled around his familiar shoulder. He whispered that everyone was watching us, so we'd better dance well. I laughed, excited to be here with him. I never thought I'd have this chance again. We knew how each other moved, and I trusted him to guide me where I needed to be. He swung me out, and I followed his lead. Here we were in plain sight. I wanted us to behave like what we were, a couple dancing at a party. We took a break. Drink. Dance. Drink.

The next time Fernando pulled me out, I wobbled as I stepped onto the cement. Every other face became a blur. I pulled him closer and laid my head on his shoulder.

"Compartarte bien," he said harshly. Behave yourself. The teachers at the Children's Center said that phrase ten times a day. Now I was angry. We'd already had this fight two, five, maybe ten times before. He would tell me that my behavior disrespected him. I would tell him that in my country, men didn't tell women how to act. Of course every boyfriend I'd ever had told me how to act, but I didn't want him to know that. On this night, I did not want to fight.

"Besa me," I said. My face was inches from his. His feet stopped moving. I was daring him to kiss me. Right there. I wanted him to show everyone that we were together. To show them the rumors were true. To show the whole town he was mine. He looked me in the eyes, leaned in and hesitated a moment before kissing me. Not a passionate, deep kiss that made me want to pull him back to my room. Just a quick peck on the lips. I couldn't believe he did it. I pulled back and looked at him. Even in my drunken haze, I knew we had crossed a line. We finished dancing to the song, but our movements were heavy and awkward. My mouth filled with saliva, and I knew I'd be sick before too long.

"I'm going back to my house," I whispered in his ear when the song ended. He didn't tell me to stop or wait. Ximenita was still sitting at the table watching us. He walked off. Ximenita started to say my name, but I held up my hand and told her I was leaving. I did not want to talk to her. I wanted to be alone. I stepped quickly to the door, already angry with myself for what I'd done. The girl at the front gate narrowed her eyes as I passed. The streets were empty as I walked the five blocks back to my house. Except for the night bus rumbling outside the bar, there was no one out.

Vergüenza. A beautiful word for the ugly shame I felt. The day after the dance, my head and heart throbbed with pain and shame. The pain in my head from drinking all night was nothing compared to the embarrassment I felt for the way I'd acted. I cringed when I thought about that kiss on the dance floor. *Todo el mundo se conoce.* Everyone knows. I started to rationalize it. Telling myself that all I'd done was ask my boyfriend for one tiny public display of affection. No big thing. But of course, I knew that was a lie. I did not want to remember, but I did. I left the Children's Center in the afternoon. To hide. I crawled into my mosquito net, pulled the blanket over my head, and tried to rest. But the dance and the kiss kept playing over and over in my mind. I wondered if I'd ever see Fernando again.

In the evening, I left my apartment to look for food. I hoped the darkness would protect me. Mercifully, Tica's hot dog stand outside the bar was open. The hot dogs popped and sizzled on the hot plate as she fried them.

Walking home from the hot dog stand, I clutched my warm and greasy paper bag to my chest. Two children stood looking at me from inside the wide-open front of the store. The boy almost looked like Fernando, I thought. Then my dehydrated brain made the connection. Those were his children. The boy was maybe four years old and had the shiny black hair and eyes of his father. I could imagine what Fernando must have looked like as a child, running around these same streets. The girl had long, straight black hair and a rounded face. She looked so much like her mother that I stopped in the middle of street. A truck trying to get by honked, and I was startled. I always knew that these children existed, but to see them was something else. Their mother had to be nearby.

"La señorita," I heard the girl say. I was surprised that she knew who I was. Then I saw Fernando's wife. Doña Luiza. Her round-cheeked face appeared from behind the door. She stood still and looked directly at me. I turned away and walked faster.

All I wanted to do was disappear into my little apartment three blocks away. Tonight, I just wanted to read a two-month-old *Newsweek* magazine and bite into that salty Bolivian hot dog. Reaching the streetlight illuminating the road in front of my apartment, I exhaled, knowing I was a few steps from invisibility.

"Señorita?" I heard behind me. She was so close. My heart was simultaneously exploding and shrinking.

"Sí?" I squeaked, turning slowly. This was it. She was going to yell at me, make a scene, and humiliate me here on the dusty cobblestone street a few feet from the safety of my bedroom. My fists clenched, and I winced with the pain I imagined she was about to lay on me. I saw her face, so close now. Those dark eyes I remembered from that rainy day last year when she brought in my laundry from the line. Dark semicircles ringed the bottom of her eyes.

"Can I speak to you about my husband?" Then I saw the kids standing behind her, peeking around her hips. The shame chilled me, spreading down from my shoulders to my arms. Her pregnant stomach extended out into the space between us. She was well into her final trimester with his next child.

"Are you my husband's lover?" she asked. I froze, incredulous that she started with this. The directness left me speechless. It sounded like something a soap opera character would say. But I heard it for the straightforward accusation it was. I swallowed. My mouth was dry.

"No," I started to say. But I could not lie to her face. "You'll have to ask him," I said and shrugged my shoulders. She was calm, no tears, no drama, simply asking me questions. A truck rumbled by at the end of the street. The daughter looked straight at me, then down at the ground. No matter what doña Luiza asked, I repeated, "You'll have to ask him." Trying to skate a narrow path between not incriminating myself and not lying.

"I heard what happened at the dance last night. I guess you had to find someone after Daniel left," she said, with the first hint of anger. She didn't know that Daniel and I were only friends or that Fernando and I had been together for several months. I was not about to correct her.

Sentences began to pop into my head: "But he said you two weren't really together anymore" or "I didn't mean for it to go on this long" or even, "But this is Latin America; doesn't every husband cheat?"

Sentences that would be an excuse. Another way of saying, "I'm not a bad person." I thought of the picture on my grandmother's dresser of me when I was crowned "Class Sweetheart" in high school. How did I get from there to here? This was not the person I thought I was. In that moment, I accepted that the least I could do for her was to be honest about the relationship. The absolute least.

"Of course, he's going to be with you if you let him," she said.

Her eyes bulged a little, and she seemed frustrated. "As women, it is our responsibility to make him behave." Our responsibility? So this was her appeal to me. This was starting to sound like something my own grandmother might say. For most of my life I believed that men couldn't help what they did and weren't responsible for their actions, especially when it came to women and girls. If men were not responsible, then the woman's behavior was at fault.

"You are disrespecting me." She placed her hands on her hips. I shrugged my shoulders and opened my palms upwards. I did not anticipate this. Above us, bugs and moths crashed into the glass of the streetlamp, drawn in by the yellow light.

Maybe I would have done the same thing as she. If I were with someone who was cheating on me, I would probably go to the other woman and try to connect with her. Try to get her to see me as a person and a woman. To understand the implications of her actions. Fernando was the one who had made a commitment to her that he was breaking. I wasn't responsible for his behavior. But I was responsible for my own behavior. How immature I had been. Playing a game that wasn't a game—not for doña Luiza or for the children. This affair connected her with me in a strange way. We both put up with him because he gave us something we wanted. We shared the affections of a flawed human.

"I am leaving Kantuta in one month," I blurted out. I hoped it would calm her.

"Are you going to take him back to the United States with you?" Her voice quivered, just a little, barely noticeable, but I heard it. In that moment, with a child growing inside her and two more depending on her, fidelity took on a different meaning.

"No, you're the lucky one who stays here with him." I used the word *luck* even though I knew this kind of luck was tangled and complicated. She was both lucky and unlucky. Lucky that he was going to stay. A single mother was more ostracized than the wife of a philanderer in this small Bolivian town. Unlucky to live in a society where a husband who cheats was tolerated and even expected. She was quiet. She needed him to stay with her. To be a husband and father, imperfect though he may have been. I also needed him to stay with his family. Homewrecker was not a role I wanted to add to my identity. By staying, he would confirm that he was not a bad person. That the man I had grown to love over the last nine months was not completely worthless.

She rubbed the side of her stomach. The little boy grabbed her hand and pulled, urging her to leave. She stood for a moment, looking at me. Maybe she was trying to decide what else to say. I felt raw and exposed, and hoped she wouldn't say anything else because I might start crying. Nodding her head toward me, she wished me good night.

"Adios," I said softly. She turned up the street she had come down, holding her son's and daughter's hands.

I took a few steps toward my front door and quickly opened it. I stood in the darkness on the other side and listened to the sound of their feet on the cobblestones. The engine of the night bus, the same one I would ride in a few weeks, revved in the background. The hot dogs were cold now, but the knot in my stomach blocked out any appetite I had. Sinking down onto my butt in the dark, I felt the cold, hard cement. This was a mess. I wished Daniel was still around so I could confide in someone. Although, at this point, sympathy for poor, horny Ursula was in short supply, and he might applaud doña Luiza for what she did.

Even as I replayed the confrontation with his wife over in my head, it was impossible for me to regret my relationship with

Fernando. I had needed human connection, and that was exactly what he gave me. Had any of this to do with my being an American Indian representing a white institution in an Indigenous country? Maybe, maybe not. I had been incredibly lonely partly because of my identity. Most volunteers felt lonely and isolated, but there was a special kind of isolation I felt being surrounded by Bolivians. They were familiar in many ways, but we were not the same.

As for the affair, that was one of the whitest things I had ever done in my life. I was living a romance novel about a hot brown dude having a passionate and illicit romance with a good white lady. Here, I was the good white lady. Back in the States, I was the brown person in the scenario. During college when my Apache/Mexican boyfriend left me for a white girl, there was no question in my mind about why he chose her over me. Or why the white guy who only dated Asian girls asked me out.

I loved Fernando, and there were moments when I wished he were single. I fantasized about taking him home to the United States, about the gorgeous multilingual, tricultural babies we'd have. But things were rocky enough outside the bedroom that I knew his commitments in Bolivia were saving me from a relationship that wouldn't last. And as all mistresses know, once a cheater, always a cheater. I could never trust him to be faithful. When I took him home that first night, trust was the last thing I cared about.

I slunk up to my room and crawled into the cold and messy bed. After trying unsuccessfully to sleep, I threw back the covers, turned on the light, and sat back down at the table to finish my Description of Service. Maybe this newfound clarity would help me write an honest account.

19
Casa — Home

Ximenita's birthday was in mid-August, the day before mine. In the US, August birthdays came in the hottest part of summer, days before school was to start. But here in the Southern Hemisphere, an August birthday fell during the coolest part of the year. Maybe that's why I forgot it was her birthday until that morning. I was standing in front of the bathroom mirror brushing my teeth when I remembered. I needed to think of something for her.

I had forgotten about both our birthdays. There were a few other things on my mind. Two weeks had passed since I had last seen Fernando. At night I heard someone knocking on my door, only to open it and see no one. Ximenita had seen me kiss Fernando in front of the whole town. She wanted to know more. It was probably killing her not to ask me a million questions. And I wanted to tell her everything, to sit in a quiet corner and share every secret I'd kept for months. How I'd fallen in love with him even though I knew it was wrong. She still believed in romance and might understand.

Teresa, by contrast, did not. When I told her about what had happened at the dance and on the street afterward, I knew she wanted to scold me. She was always rational and smart, tucking the corner of her mouth up into her cheek in a look that I knew meant, "I told you so."

After his wife's surprise confrontation in the street, I didn't know whether I'd see Fernando before I left in a few weeks. I wanted to see him, but knew I shouldn't. I tried not to think about him, but flashes of his smirking face, or the way he said my name, kept coming into my brain. Seeing him might be too risky. I heard a murmur in the patio and realized my neighbor's housekeeper had turned the radio on while she washed clothes in the patio sink. My stomach tensed. It was Fernando, reading announcements in Quechua. His voice was flat and normal. Because it was in Quechua, I understood only a few words. Someone was selling livestock. The housekeeper never turned on the radio in the mornings. Was she doing this because she knew? I was not going to show that it affected me. I wanted to stand and listen to his voice, but walked out the door.

Tomas and Umberto were waiting for me when I arrived at the Children's Center that day. I had promised to take them to the store to buy each of them gifts. The pretext was a missed birthday or holiday, but really I wanted to give them something to remember me by. These brothers had almost no belongings beyond their faded jeans and sandals. At lunch, I had seen Tomas stare at a little boy playing with a small black toy car. None of these kids had much of anything, and a toy car was a big deal for any of them. It broke my heart to see him look with such longing at the toy. With the blessing of the Children's Center director, the boys and I walked to the nearest store during our lunch break. I told the boys they could have any one thing they wanted. Their choice.

Umberto, who was almost nine, quickly walked to the corner where boxes of shoes were stacked against the wall. He was practical, rational. He found a pair of new shoes. Tomas picked up a shirt, then put it down. Then he picked up a toy and put it down. Each time I asked if that was what he wanted. He was silent. Finally, he walked up with a baseball cap that was too big for his little head. For the third time, the store owner asked if we were ready. Normally, this man would have followed them around, assuming they might steal something. But because I was escorting them and paying for the purchases, he knew he had to treat them differently. Tomas looked at me with wide eyes. A baseball cap? Of everything in the store, he wanted a two-dollar baseball cap? This little boy who owned nothing in the world but old sandals made from tires that barely held together and a collection of stained shirts wanted an oversized baseball cap?! It didn't make sense to me. Why did he want that? But I had promised to let them choose. The total price came to less than ten dollars, about fifty bolivianos. I felt benevolent and generous. Like Oprah. The brothers and I walked out of the store, and Umberto thanked me. They asked if they could run ahead because they didn't want to miss lunch.

It was very satisfying…for about a minute. I wondered whether I was being unfair to the other children. I couldn't afford to buy something for everyone. Charity was complicated. When people like me had so much, could give so much without even noticing it, what did it mean? Umberto and Tomas were sweet boys, and I felt sorry for them. But I hated for people to feel sorry for me. Because I had no father and was raised by a single mother, my life seemed pitiable to many. I heard it in the voices of my teachers or the nurses at the Indian health clinic. Charity can dehumanize the recipient even as it bolsters the ego of the giver. It is difficult to do charity right, in a way that isn't insulting. I wasn't sure I was doing it right.

Ximenita told me I could buy her dinner. She was a cook, but never went out to dinner. I was grateful to have someone to eat with. Since Daniel left, my dinners were usually a tomato sandwich eaten alone in my room. Fernando and I could not go out to eat, and my female Bolivian friends never went to restaurants. Ximenita seemed excited as we walked toward the center of town to choose a restaurant. Dinner and a thank you for being my friend for the last two years.

"Have you heard from Fernando since the night of the dance?" she leaned across the table and asked after we ordered our food. The restaurant was nearly empty, and the TV was off. From where we were sitting, I could see out the open front door onto the street where more people than cars passed by. I hadn't told her about his wife confronting me.

"No," I answered. I was trying not to admit anything or incriminate myself. I sipped the room-temperature soda that arrived at our table. I knew she had questions about my relationship with Fernando, that she had heard rumors for months. But I didn't want to talk to her about it. She was young, and romance was more important than anything to her. A few months ago, when the relationship was singing, all I'd wanted to do was confide in her because I knew she'd let me gush. I had somehow managed to control myself then. Now I wasn't even tempted because there was nothing to gush about.

The server put two plates of fried chicken, french fries, and rice in front of us. The meat was still sizzling, and the dark fried skin was shiny with grease. I was going to miss these carbs when I returned to the US. Ximenita looked at me as she ripped chunks of the flesh off the bone with her fingers and put them into her mouth. She took a big bite of rice and grimaced.

"My rice tastes better than this," she whispered, cupping her hand next to her mouth. She covered her mouth and laughed. I rolled my eyes and laughed. Her rice *was* better. My rice was always a disaster, either watery or burned. Mostly I was grateful that she had changed the subject.

Right then a man with a cut and bloody hand stumbled into the front of the restaurant. The sleeve of his white shirt was ripped, and his pants had a dark stain near the bottom of the cuff, which I hoped was mud. His eyes were glassy. The restaurant owner walked up and asked what was the matter.

"Un accidente," the man said loudly, as though he couldn't hear his own voice. The evening bus from Cochabamba had gone off the side of the road a few miles outside town. That was the bus I usually took. The bus that everyone rode. These accidents happened a couple of times a year. Narrow dirt roads cut into steep hills sometimes gave way, especially during the rainy season. Sometimes the drivers were drinking or fell asleep at the wheel. You had to accept the risks if you were traveling in Bolivia. The man stumbled out the door and walked off in the direction of the clinic.

Ximenita thanked me for buying her dinner. The reminder of death had ruined any light conversation we might have had. We kissed each other's cheeks, and she hugged my shoulders. I gave her an extra squeeze. She turned and strutted up toward the Children's Center.

I wished I could have gone back to that first day in Bolivia, when I felt overlooked by the man at the airport, and tell myself that the connection I wanted would come with time. No one, not even an olive-skinned American Indian, would be granted an instant connection. The similarities in our heritage put the pressure on me, not them. When I arrived in Bolivia, I thought that being Native meant that they would see me differently. But like everyone else, I had to build their trust one meeting, one project, one bucket of chicha at a time. Two years of service had once seemed like forever. Now it seemed barely enough time to get everyone to believe you were who you said you were.

I stepped out of the restaurant and could hardly bear to look across the street at the half-dark road leading to my house. The door to my little room—the tiny space on the first floor that I had chosen because it gave Fernando easy access to me—was in shadow, but I knew the room was there. Empty and messy, it was not where I wanted to go. I heard a telephone ring as I crossed in front of the telephone store. I decided to call my mom. Maybe the news from home would rev me up for my impending departure.

Dark wood chairs lined the walls of the large empty room. An older cholita, her sandaled feet barely touching the floor, sat alone on a bench inside. Behind a large desk in the corner sat a teenage boy, dialing numbers and pointing customers to small rooms where the telephones sat. There were two telephone lines, and customers had to wait until a line opened up. Calling the United States cost fifty cents per minute, due immediately in cash. Even if no one was home, this was at least a dollar, usually two. I handed the boy my mother's telephone number and sat down on the bench. The cholita met my eyes, and a quick smile crossed her face. I nodded back and kicked my legs out in front of me to relax. The boy dialed all the numbers and then motioned with his chin to the closet that functioned as a phone booth. In the big cities, these telephone stores had clear Plexiglas booths that were amazingly soundproof. Here it was just a room with a glass door.

I picked up the phone and immediately relaxed as my mother said, "Hello, dear. Happy early birthday." She told me about all of my family in Oregon and California. I listened, wondering what it would be like to be back there in a few weeks, looking for work and a place to live. She paused after a few minutes.

"And how are you doing?" she asked. I prepared to launch into an explanation about wrapping up my service and saying good-bye to my friends, about my plans to travel in South America before returning home. All the shiny, smart plans that made me sound like the bright girl I wanted everyone to think I was. Especially my mom, who was so proud that I hadn't followed her path to single motherhood and no college degree until she was in her forties.

"Not so great, Mom." I was too tired and heartbroken to pretend I wasn't. I decided to tell her the truth. But I knew I had to start at the beginning. "I've been having an affair with a married man, a Bolivian." She didn't say anything, and I couldn't tell whether the crackling I heard was her breath or the poor connection stretching from the heart of Bolivia to Oregon. I gave her enough details so that she knew it had been going on for almost the whole year. From where I stood, I could see the boy at his desk. If he wanted to, he could pick up the receiver and listen to what I was saying. If he understood English, I wouldn't be telling this story.

"His wife confronted me in the street, asking me about the affair."

"What did you do?"

"What could I do? I am a terrible liar, so I admitted the truth." I told her. My mother was silent. The cholita in the office said something in Quechua to the teenager behind the desk.

"Please be careful, honey. You only have a couple more weeks." She said something else, but I couldn't hear it. The connection was deteriorating. We made plans to talk again when I was in La Paz and we could have a long conversation.

"Don't worry about me, Mom. I'm going to be OK," I told her. My voice cracked a little, but I knew she wouldn't be able to hear the change in my tone. I hung up and walked out of the phone booth. The cholita was still sitting at the same place on the bench, waiting patiently for her phone call. The boy asked me for forty Bolivianos, about eight dollars.

I hadn't told my mom about my relationship with Fernando before this moment. I liked to tell her about things that would make her proud. Much of the time, I thought she would not understand anything about my life here. Yet, as I stood in that phone booth, I remembered a guy my mom dated when I was in high school. She thought this guy looked like a Native Eric Estrada. I was fifteen and hated him because I hated that town and missed my friends in Oregon. She was one of the only Native women in the offices of the Bureau of Indian Affairs serving the Quinault reservation in far western Washington State. Her coworkers were mostly white men. On the rez, she inspected the work of loggers. Most of them were white guys who were notoriously rough and disrespectful to Native women. She'd left Oregon for a job with the Bureau of Indian Affairs because it offered good pay, good benefits, and an opportunity to finish college. She was a Native woman representing a white organization serving Native people, who connected with a Native man. Just like me. I took comfort in the same places my mother took comfort.

Was this a Native thing? How could the relationship have been both a Native thing and the whitest, most privileged thing I had ever done? Because I was both white and Native—especially here. Privileged and unprivileged. The Bolivians saw me as a white Westerner despite the tribal ID card in my wallet. My relative wealth, my lack of connection to the community, my connection to the US government—all these things gave me privilege. But I never stopped feeling like a Native. I never stopped being a Karuk. I never forgot that compared to most of the other volunteers, I was poor, had no connections to power, and would return to those conditions the day I landed back in Miami.

I tripped across the street, narrowly avoiding someone on a bike. He rang his bell at me, but I ignored him, lost in my thoughts. In a few hours, it would be my birthday. Happy Birthday, girl.

Back in my room, I sat down at the cluttered table that served as my writing desk and dining room. A half-empty bottle of water, a stack of unread *Newsweek* magazines, Maya Angelou's book *All God's Children Need Traveling Shoes*, and a small photo album with recently developed pictures covered the brown tabletop. Too much to carry with me out of Kantuta. I needed to give some of this stuff away. I started a pile of things I could live without and things that I needed to survive the next step in my life. Jodi and I had finally decided to meet up in Salvador de Bahía, Brazil, a few weeks after our service ended. I imagined us sucking down sweet drinks on the beach and acting like tourists while a shirtless buff man performed capoeira in the sand next to me. I had no idea what Brazil would be like, but I retreated to these fantasizes when the reality of my messy life felt overwhelming. Sorting gave me something to do.

Sometime after midnight, there was a knock on my door. I had fallen asleep with the light on. I lifted my head, but wasn't sure if I'd heard it or dreamed it. There it was again, unmistakable.

"Feliz cumpleaños, mi amor," Fernando said as he entered the room and kissed me. He ignored the shocked look on my face. He had promised to visit me on my birthday, but with everything that had happened, I didn't expect him.

"Your wife, she…," I stepped back and started to say.

"I know," he interrupted, picking up the photo book from my pile of things to keep. "Tell me—why did you tell her about us?" he asked.

"I couldn't lie," I said. He narrowed his eyes and pressed his lips together as though there was something he wanted to say but couldn't.

"Your words caused me a mountain of problems," he said as he thumbed through the photos. There was a picture of him in there. A memento I let myself keep. I explained what she said and what I said, pacing back and forth in front of the door. I knew he shouldn't be there. I finished talking and stood there staring at him. He put the photo album down and sighed as he looked at me. Seven months ago when we slipped through my front door, neither of us had any idea that we'd be standing here, two weeks before my departure, talking about my conversation with his wife. What a mess.

He stepped closer. It was cold, and he was wearing a thick knitted sweater. Not the alpaca kind that tourists buy in the street markets of La Paz, the kind I bought two years ago. He had on a regular old warm knitted sweater that Bolivians wore. This might be the last time I would ever see him. I reached out and touched his chest. The fabric was soft and thick. He pulled out a small box from his pocket, something wrapped in a bow. A birthday gift? A going-away gift? A consolation prize?

"Un recuerdo," he said. I opened the little box to find a slim chain necklace. Small and shiny, it looked too delicate for me. He stood behind me and connected the two ends of the necklace. I pressed it into my chest and thanked him. I had expected an argument. But he did not seem interested in rehashing what had happened. And even though I had been thinking about it for the last two weeks, I did not want to spend this moment arguing. It was my birthday, and he was here. I turned and faced him. There was that horrible sweet cologne of his.

We ended the relationship the way we began it: in my bed. I cried a little, not a lot. We made promises to stay in touch that I knew weren't true even as I whispered the words. I missed him already, but I was done being the girl who waits. I was ready to move on. Everything was slow and deliberate that night because I wanted to remember it all. He left before the sun came up.

The next day, as I listened to him read the news on Radio Kantuta, his voice seemed scratched and rough. I felt as tired as he sounded. It was my birthday, my last in Bolivia. I had two weeks left.

20
Mi Salida — My Departure

A knock and then a gangly teenage boy was standing outside my open door. He reached out his long arm and handed me a piece of paper. *Una llamada de Daniel* was written on it. Daniel had left Kantuta three months earlier, and except for a few letters, I had not heard much from him. I had no idea why he was calling me on this day. It was less than a week before I was to leave Kantuta.

"From Daniel?" I asked the boy, confirming that the message was correct. He scrunched up his face in an expression that was either boredom or nervousness.

"Sí, una llamada de Daniel, el gringo de los Estados Unidos, a señorita Ursula," he motioned for me to follow him. That was me, señorita Ursula.

Knocks on the door were more frequent now than ever. But now it was friends stopping by to say good-bye. Or people wondering whether I needed anyone to take that stove, blender, or table off my hands. I was the fourth volunteer to leave this town in the last few years, and those who'd seen these departures before knew we couldn't take much of anything back to the States.

I wasn't sure why Daniel was calling me, but after everything we'd been through, if he was calling, I was going to answer. The boy pedaled slowly on his too-small bike and led me to the telephone office by the plaza across the street from where Daniel used to live. Now that Daniel wasn't there anymore, I rarely came over to this side of town. The church stood guard over the dusty central plaza. The hedges were trimmed, and the trees didn't look as droopy as I remembered. The leaves of the tall palm trees rustled in the breeze, sounding like rain, but the day was dry. The smell of fresh bread drifted from the other side of the plaza where the best rolls in town were sold.

I followed the boy inside the dim and cavernous telephone office. The hard wood bench was smooth from years of seated customers waiting for phone calls. I thought impatiently of the clothes I needed to pack or give away that sat unfolded on my table in my little room. I tapped my foot in annoyance that I was forced to sit and wait for a call. From behind a closed door came the low mumble of a man. Just as I started to become anxious, the teenager motioned for me to go into the other empty booth. I picked up the hard plastic receiver.

"Hello, darlin'," Daniel said. The lift in his voice made me smile. My breath slowed, and my shoulders relaxed. He told me about surfing again, going to the beach where he used to live. Every wave was different, a new opportunity, a new challenge. Quickly he asked about what was going on in Kantuta. Everything that had happened to me over the last two weeks came pouring out: the drunken kiss with Fernando at the dance; his wife's confrontation; how I choked up a little with every hug from a child at the Center, knowing it might be the last. He laughed.

"No me digas!" he said with a little bit too much enthusiasm. What must this fermented drama sound like to him, thousands of miles away, sitting in his parents' air-conditioned house within view of the Pacific Ocean? At least that's what I imagined. It was winter here, cold and dusty. In California, it was the warmest part of summer. I was silent for a moment. Is this what awaited me back in the United States? Would this life and my experience here become an amusing story?

From where I stood, I could see groups of young children crossing through the bright sunshine in the plaza. They wore clean white smocks and backpacks on their backs. The day was starting, and I needed to get going.

"They will become ghosts to you," Daniel said. His voice was deep and serious. Was this a warning or a lament? I didn't want it to be true. I wanted to rebel against him, to tell him that for me it would be different. Whatever he was saying, I would not hear it right then. The people of Kantuta were not ghosts to me, and the idea that I would ever think of them as ghosts scared me. But with everything that was going on, I hadn't had time to think much about what life would be like once I returned to the US. I saw myself on my grandmother's couch in San Francisco, joking with her while we drank tea and watched the local news. I wanted to cry, but stopped myself.

"Call me when you get back to the States, OK?" he said. "You'll feel kind of messed up at first, so be prepared." He was showing me the way as he had when he was here, but I resented his assumption that we had had the same experience in Kantuta.

When I finally arrived at the Children's Center, two of the younger girls led me to the cafeteria and sat me down at the head of one of the tables. The shiest girl at the Center, who always kept her eyes lowered even as her dimples popped, put a chipped porcelain bowl full of soup in front of me.

"Gracias," I said. She smiled tightly and met my eyes for only a second. *Sopa de mani*, peanut soup. Florencia and Ximenita knew what my favorite foods were and had cooked them for me. The thick white soup was salty, and I slurped it down quickly. Around me sat a row of young girls in white smocks, looking like a table of scientists about to go into the lab to perform important experiments. Marisol, the very tough little girl who spoke to me on my first day at the Center, asked me whether my family was glad that I was returning home. I told her that I thought they were and that I knew I was excited to see them. All of these girls, with their smart faces and dark hair pulled tight into bouncy ponytails, knew what it was to live apart from their family. Each of them spent the majority of the year living at this Children's Center to attend school. In a few years, these girls might be encouraged to leave school and start working to earn money to support the brothers and sisters still at home.

"Attention, attention, please," the director of the school said as he stood at the far end of the cafeteria. He rubbed his hands together, trying to get everyone to quiet down.

"Today we are honoring a special friend who has been with us for two years." I put down my soup spoon and exhaled. Keep it together, Ursula. I did not want to start crying, to have their last memory of me as a blubbering gringa.

"Over the last two years, señorita Ursula has helped us with many things, like the charango workshop and the bakery. Now we want to thank her for everything she did." He looked at me and led the cafeteria in a round of applause. The girls at my table put down their spoons and clapped for me, keeping their eyes on the director. "Does anyone want to say anything to the señorita?"

Joel, the boy who had always been helpful, the first one to make a charango in the workshop, stepped up and, ducking his head respectfully, thanked me for helping with the workshop. Tears and sobs waited anxiously behind my scrunched-up face. Rita, with her long hair pulled behind her in a braid, stood up and said thank you for teaching them about bakery businesses.

"Is there anything that you'd like to say, señorita?" the director asked. I stood and pushed the hard plastic chair behind me. Tomas, sitting at the next table, grinned his gap-toothed smile. I could not look at his face or I'd start crying.

"I…" was all I could get out before crying. In between sobs and wiping my nose, I uttered a string of words that began with "Thank you" and "Love you" and "I will miss you all." I don't know whether it made any sense or whether they could hear me above the crying, but I said it.

"Bueno." The director cleared his throat. My choking, crying good-bye must have surprised him as much as it surprised me. "Children, this is what happens when we feel strong emotions." I suddenly felt embarrassed for my outburst. I was exposed. My love for these children and the adults who cared for them was controlling me.

Ximenita and doña Florencia hugged me tightly. Florencia hugged me with her strong arms, and I forgot to cry. The boys shook my hand, respectfully thanking me. The girls hugged me and asked why I had to leave. Despite whatever I did or didn't do, they loved me and wanted me to stay. I had never imagined it would be this difficult to leave.

"Aye mamita, don't leave," said Ximenita as she held both my hands and wouldn't let me go. Finally, after more hugs and promises to write, I was released, and walked toward the gate. Stepping into the street, I felt empty, exhausted, and lighter. I remembered Rowena's question: Had it been worth it for the US government to send me here? Certainly in terms of the actual cost of my training and support versus the income generated by the Children's Center, this was not a good return on investment. When I came to Bolivia, I thought Bolivians needed saving, or at least someone to help them. The question for me then was, did I have what it took to help them? I learned that they didn't need saving. The best help we could give them was the same we could give to a community in the US, which was to ask what they needed and really listen to their answer. Then work with them to see how they wanted us to help and, we would hope, build relationships along the way. I knew that when I returned to the US, I would be encouraged to describe what I had done to help Bolivians, to put my accomplishments on a resume or in a graduate school application. Yet anything that I achieved while I was at the Children's Center was due to Teresa's help, Ximenita's support, Daniel's encouragement, and the girls in the bakery deciding to spend a few Saturday mornings kneading dough. I thought I should be ashamed that I needed their help. But really the success or failure of my two years of service was less about the projects I started or completed and more about being a part of something.

The funny thing is, I already knew that any meaningful project didn't rest on one person's shoulders. When our group of Native students from tribes across North America planned our student powwows, we were all doing it for each other. And at the end of the night, we gathered together, ate the leftover frybread, and started planning for the next year. Who am I kidding? There was never any leftover frybread, just the lettuce and tomatoes for the Indian taco toppings, and that one guy always left early. But the rest of us shared whatever we had.

I also thought differently about Nina's work at the Center. She wrote a grant that funded a workshop. Did she save anyone? No, but she did what any good employee does—her job. Her work gave me something to build off of. When I met her, I thought she was cold and aloof. But my respect for her work had increased as I learned for myself the challenges of launching a project. I also now understood how she might have felt on those last days, how difficult it was to leave Kantuta and people she loved forever.

My room was stacked with boxes ready to be loaded on the bus. I gave away everything from my kitchen including the pressure cooker that I used to make popcorn and the oven that mostly existed to make toast. Honestly, I was relieved to know that Fernando wouldn't be coming over to see me again. I was sad and tired when I thought about him, and knew I should have ended it earlier, but I had been afraid of being alone. I felt empty when I met him, and let the excitement and drama of the affair fill me up. I made him the sun at the center of my universe and altered my orbit to capture every wave of heat and light that he offered. It was time to spend time with myself for a while and bask in my own sunshine.

Lucas invited me for dinner at his house that last night. Seeing him pop through my front door to ask me over was a surprise I hadn't expected. We hadn't seen each other much in the last few months. He already knew about Fernando; I had told him months earlier. Lucas knew Fernando from a project he did at Radio Kantuta, which was a reminder of how small a town Kantuta was. Lucas and I sat in his dining room one last time, and he asked what I was going to do next. I repeated the line I had said for months. The one about graduate school, Portland, the US, and community development. It sounded good. I gave answers that sounded good. The truth was I didn't know. But in that moment, I did not want to think about it. I knew I would be OK. Lucas gave me a warm hug, a good-bye-old-friend hug, and I walked outside.

And then it was my last day. After one cup of instant coffee, I pulled the mattress and blankets out of my mosquito net. I untied the ropes holding it up. The green mass of netting collapsed into a lump of the floor. How had that pile of canvas, netting, and zippers contained so much of what had happened over the last two years? The nights I passed out or cried myself to sleep or pulled the covers up to my grinning face or invited Fernando in and kicked him out or every once in a while fell into a sound sleep after a hard day's work.

The rest of the day was a swirl of good-byes and giveaways. Two hours before I was to leave, the bus to Cochabamba squealed to a stop on the side road in front of my apartment. A few teenagers from the Center showed up. Then the director; his wife, doña Florencia; and four of their children also arrived. Twenty adults and children lined the walls of my tiny pink bedroom. Teresa walked in with her son, and I wondered where I had packed my toilet paper, because I knew I would be crying soon. It was difficult to move, difficult to hear everyone, but I knew I was loved. I tried to give everyone something, even if it was only a used pot for boiling water. I wondered whether they had done this for Nina, but then decided I didn't care; they were here for me, and that's what mattered.

"It isn't much, but I wanted you to have this," Teresa said as she handed me a woven wall hanging of a cholita with an *aguayo* walking toward a snow-covered mountain. It was the perfect representation of everything I thought I would find when I arrived in Bolivia—one-dimensional, simple stereotypes in front of idyllic landscapes. Teresa sniffled, and I hugged her. This woman had not only welcomed me into her home and her life but also patiently explained Bolivian culture to me when I didn't understand what was going on. Her mother, her brothers and their wives, and even her grandmother, who didn't speak a word of Spanish, all treated me like a member of the family. The bakery project would never have existed without her help. What I appreciated most was her honesty. She was like Laura in that way, not afraid to tell me when she disagreed with me, but remaining my friend. Teresa had done more for me than I ever did for her.

"Tell your mother and your brothers good-bye for me," I said. I didn't know whether I would ever see her again. I promised myself that I would stay in touch with her, but remembered what Daniel had said about these people becoming ghosts.

Simon handed me a leather picture frame he had engraved. His wife, doña Florencia, gave me a weaving, and I stuck both into the top of my backpack. I hadn't expected this generosity, and although I was tired and distracted, I wanted them all to know I appreciated their gifts. Everyone followed me into the street and helped carry my backpack, duffle bag, and boxes to the boys loading suitcases onto the top of the bus. The driver honked the horn, and I stepped onto the bus.

After crying for a week straight, I had no more tears left. My friends and the children from the Center stood on the street waving good-bye and blowing kisses. I placed my open palm on the window. I leaned back in my seat as the bus crossed the tiny bridge on the northern edge of town and tottered up the hill by the Candelaria bull ring. I was tempted to look for Fernando. Part of me hoped he would be hiding on a side street, waiting to wave to me as the bus passed. But I didn't look because I didn't want to see that he wasn't there.

From the day I arrived in Bolivia, I wanted Bolivians to see me and to understand that I was an Indigenous person like them. But I was the one who needed to see *them*. I was the one coming to their country, to their community, with wealth and privilege. I was the one who needed to prove myself to them. I should have already known this, considering all the times I saw outsiders come into a Native community and assume that because they professed respect and love for Native people, they would be immediately accepted. "I'm one of the good ones," they said. I thought I was one of the "good" North Americans, but I needed to prove it.

The next morning was Thursday. It would dawn exactly as every other Thursday had during my two years in Kantuta. The garbage truck would rumble through the streets near my room. The grumpy mailman would slowly sort through his recently arrived mail. And at the Children's Center, they would roll out the dough to make enough bread to last the week.

Afterword

Kantuta isn't the real name of the Bolivian town where I lived for two years. I changed the name of the town, as well as the names of the people, for this book because I'm the only one who should be identified in this story. That town is not the same place today as it was when I left in 1996. The streets are wider and mostly paved. Hills that had nothing but brush and narrow foot trails now have homes built on them. A new highway into town turned the seven-hour trip from Cochabamba into a quick four-hour ride.

Ironically, much of the change occurred because of a massive earthquake that hit Kantuta in the middle of the night in 1998. I found out about the earthquake when Daniel called me early the morning after. He was flying to Bolivia to see what he could do. I wished I could go with him, but was about to start graduate school and couldn't afford it. That familiar feeling of being tempted to follow Daniel on an adventure sprung up even though we hadn't spoken in months. When he returned from his trip, he described Kantuta to me. The church spire fell into the main plaza, and homes made of adobe and rock crumbled into dust. Nearly a hundred people died, and everyone moved into the streets to live under blue tarps as aftershocks rocked the ground. None of the Bolivians named in this book died in the earthquake, but all of them were impacted by the destruction it brought. Many people I knew had a mother, sister, husband, or child die that night.

Bolivia still has the largest percentage of Indigenous people of any country in South America. In 2006, Bolivians elected their first Indigenous president, Evo Morales. The election of an Aymara coca farmer as president made it seem as though the world was changing. I thought of the times I heard someone use *Indio* as an insult and hoped the election meant things were changing for Bolivia's Indigenous population. Evo became a celebrity, and nowhere was he more celebrated than in the Native community in the United States. Every time Evo said something supporting Indigenous people or had a meeting with other Indigenous leaders, it popped up in an online Native forum or newspaper. I have shared and "hearted" hundreds of tweets and social media posts about Evo over the years.

Evo brought dramatic changes to Bolivia. Many of his accomplishments focused on recognizing the value of the country's Indigenous population. A new constitution made the country's thirty-seven Indigenous languages official national languages for the first time. Other changes, such as nationalizing foreign companies making money from gas and oil resources, grew the country's economy. Because of the many programs his administration implemented, within a few years Bolivians were more educated and living longer than they had been before, and poverty had declined.

The US ambassador was asked to leave by Evo's administration in 2008, and soon afterward the Peace Corps closed up shop and left. Volunteers had to gather their things and return to the capital city a few days later to catch a flight back to the United States. I have always had questions about the value of Peace Corps volunteers, and because of that, I wasn't convinced that their departure was a bad thing. I understood the significance of kicking the gringos out even though I know those volunteers probably hated having to leave that way. If I had been evacuated like that, I would have been angry. Although, honestly, I would also have loved to be a volunteer in Evo's Bolivia to witness the changes taking place at the community level and in the lives of my friends.

In 2018, I returned to Bolivia with my husband, who is also a former Peace Corps volunteer. Images of Evo's face were everywhere, spanning the sides of buildings next to the words "With Evo We Have a Future" painted in light blue. A picture of Evo smiling in a hard hat loomed over the entrance to Mi Telferico, the newly built aerial trams that move tourists and commuters above the jammed streets of La Paz. In the countryside, I saw his picture next to covered soccer courts, called *canchas*, that double as community centers. A person didn't have to read Spanish or Quechua to get the message, "This was brought to you by Evo."

Millions of Bolivians across the country were learning how to read and write in Quechua, Aymara, and other Indigenous languages because of education reforms Evo's government put into place. One night at a pizza restaurant on the Prado in Cochabamba, the young children at the table next to us counted to ten in Quechua when their parents asked them what they had learned at school. Indigenous languages across the world are lost every day, and hearing them spoken and seeing them taught made me hopeful for the future of Bolivia. I lament that I can speak only a few words of my own tribe's language.

In 2019, despite constitutional term limits and a national referendum against him, Evo ran for president again. He won even though there were questions about election interference and demands for a new election. But he resigned the presidency a week later after suggestions from the military that he should leave. Massive protests for and against Evo paralyzed the country after his resignation. Several protestors were killed in street demonstrations. The Bolivians I know have described the situation as grave, and they wonder what will happen to their country.

Still, it was clear that the concept of an Indigenous identity had evolved in Bolivia in the time since I left South America. I asked as many Bolivians as I dared whether they considered themselves Indigenous. I never would have had the courage to ask this when I lived there. It's a question an anthropologist would ask, which made me uncomfortable. I'd start by first telling them that I was Indigenous. *Indígena* and *mestizo* were the terms they used. Without hesitation, they all said they considered themselves Aymara or Quechua or, like the majority of US Natives, a mix of groups with Native and non-Native backgrounds. One thing that hadn't changed was the power of the word *Indio*. *Indio* means Indian, but it implies poverty, lack of education, dark skin, and other qualities that few Bolivians want to claim. Despite the charts showing a growing economy, the Indigenous people of Bolivia are still the poorest. Income inequality remains a problem, and the Indigenous people are at the bottom. Average Bolivians may feel more comfortable about their Indigenous identity, but every time I used the word

Indio, I was corrected and asked to use *Indígena* instead.

My understanding of my Indigenous identity has also evolved. Before, it was something I kept to myself as much as possible. I wasn't hiding, only trying to avoid stereotypes. Now I'm more likely to share it with non-Native people, and I understand that I am part of the diversity of North American Indians that I witnessed as a kid.

There has also been little change in how people talk about Westerners traveling to the developing world to help. When I first understood the term *white savior*, I knew it was referring to those Westerners with no training trying to help the "poor" black and brown people. In Teju Cole's essay "The White-Savior Industrial Complex," he states, "The White Savior Industrial Complex is not about justice. It is about having a big emotional experience that validates privilege." That's exactly what my big emotional experience did. And those saviors haven't stopped. On my return flight from Bolivia, I sat next to a woman coming back from a mission trip to Haiti, who was very pleased about the church she helped build and that she had been able to do God's work while also getting a tan on a "safe" beach. When I overhear someone humble-bragging about joining Peace Corps, I can't help but notice that it is usually a white person with a tone in his voice giving away how much he hopes to save people.

After Peace Corps, I entered a graduate school program and served as an AmeriCorps volunteer in rural Illinois. AmeriCorps pays a few thousand dollars at the end a volunteer's service, and I needed that money to help pay down my student loans. I noticed something about AmeriCorps that was different from Peace Corps: many more black, brown, and Asian faces. In AmeriCorps, white people are the minority. Why is that? I can't speak for the whole organization, but my AmeriCorps service was presented as an opportunity to learn about community development rather than to save anyone. There was no weirdness about whether I was really helping anyone. The program appealed to my urge to serve while recognizing the financial reality that I had to pay for my degree. I've wondered whether anyone at Peace Corps recognizes these differences. To me they are obvious.

The most satisfying part of returning to Kantuta was seeing the people I knew. The Children's Center still stands, but it is empty, having lost its international sponsors. Teresa, the Bolivian teacher whom I met at the Children's Center, still lives on the corner near the market. Twenty-five years later, I realize that the most important relationships I had were with her and Ximenita. They helped me survive my bad choices and the isolation I felt in that little town. On my return trip, we stayed at Teresa's house. Teresa finished college and earned her teaching degree. Her son, the little boy who ran around while she cut and colored my hair, graduated with a degree in business and works in Cochabamba. There are still tough times, and Teresa's brothers have difficulty finding work, but many of her nieces and nephews are going to college. Tomas, the gap-toothed little boy, has a wife and two small children. He works at a bank, and both he and his brother, Umberto, still live in Kantuta.

Toward the end of my return trip, we visited the school in the countryside where Teresa now teaches. She translated everything we said to her students from Spanish into Quechua. They were also learning English, and she asked us to teach her students a song. We sang "Mary Had a Little Lamb" three times. Most of the kids sitting in that room had sheep or goats, so having one follow you to school one day was a real-world problem they could relate to. In return, the kids sang the Bolivian national anthem. Two decades earlier, I had learned the anthem for our official entry into service. I recognized the melody even though I had forgotten many of the words. The final line of the song is the only one I remembered:

Morir antes que esclavos vivir.

We will die before living as slaves.

I had always loved the boldness of that line. *Resilience* is an overused word when it comes to Indigenous people, but that line about slaves reminds me of the resilience of Bolivians. The Bolivians I know are strong and funny. Every morning at every school, at the beginning of every soccer game, and for a hundred other reasons every week, they remind themselves.

Morir antes que esclavos vivir.

In Bolivia's October 2020 election, Evo Morales's party won and his handpicked successor became the next president. I hope this means that Bolivia will return to some version of normal and that my friends can raise their children in a country that recognizes the importance of the Quechua, Aymara, Guarani, and all the Indigenous populations.

I hope this book will open up opportunities for black, Indigenous, and other people of color to publish their Peace Corps stories. I've seen the blogs and social media posts of beautiful black and brown faces serving across the world, and I wanted to read books about those volunteers and their experiences.

Acknowledgments

Thank you Charlotte Gullick and the Creative Writing Department at Austin Community College for giving me an opportunity to share my writing with others for the first time, as well as the librarians at every ACC campus for providing a quiet place to hide away and write.

This book would never have been written if I hadn't attended the MFA program at the Institute for American Indian Arts in Santa Fe. Thank you to my instructors Chip Livingston, Melissa Febos, and Elissa Washuta for gently and honestly guiding my writing. Thank you to my fellow IAIA alums for sharing your stories and encouraging me to tell my story. During my time at IAIA, the American Indian Graduate Center helped support me, and I'm grateful for that.

Thank you Heyday and the Berkeley Roundhouse for seeing the value in my story, specifically Marthine Satris for your kindness and patience, and editors Emmerich Anklam and Terria Smith. You showed me great respect and provided the crucial advice and suggestions that made this the best book it could be. Thanks to copyeditor Michele Jones for your attention to detail.

I thank the Writers' League of Texas, and the community of

writers in Texas who helped me navigate the path from MFA to publication.

Gracias y pachi a Bety, Calixta, y la gente de la comunidad tan querida en Bolivia donde yo vivía por dos años. Mil gracias a Sergio, Elmer, David, y todos los niños del Centro Infantil.

My experience in Bolivia wouldn't have been the same without the friendships of Kasey, Jeff, Jennifer, and the other volunteers who served with me. Thank you all.

Thank you to my husband, Kenn, for always being supportive of me while I wrote this book, and to my children, Marisol and Armando, for listening to a thousand stories about Bolivia. I would never have gone to Bolivia without my mother's encouragement. Thank you auntie Betty for sending me a stack of blank journals to fill with my story.

Yôotva to my Karuk family, my ancestors, and all the Karuk people using old and new ways to keep our language and culture alive.

About the Author

URSULA PIKE is a graduate of the MFA program at the Institute of American Indian Arts. Her work won the 2019 Writers' League of Texas Manuscript Contest in the memoir category, and her writing has appeared in *Yellow Medicine Review*, *World Literature Today*, and *Ligeia Magazine*. She has an MA in economics, with a focus on community economic development, and was a Peace Corps fellow at Western Illinois University. She served as a Peace Corps volunteer in Bolivia from 1994 to 1996. An enrolled member of the Karuk Tribe, she was born in California and grew up in Daly City, California, and Portland, Oregon. She currently lives in Austin, Texas.